MW01156642

A–Z

of

Needlepoint

SEARCH PRESS

Contents

Take your needle, my child, and work at your pattern; it will come out a rose by and by. Life is like that – one stitch at a time taken patiently and the pattern will come out all right like the embroidery.

Oliver Wendell Holmes

First published in Great Britain 2015

Search Press Limited
Wellwood, North Farm Road,
Tunbridge Wells, Kent TN2 3DR

First published in Australia by
Country Bumpkin Publications
© Country Bumpkin Publications

All rights reserved. No part of
this book, text, photographs or
illustrations may be reproduced
or transmitted in any form or by
any means by print, photoprint,
microfilm, microfiche, photocopier,
internet or in any way known or as
yet unknown, or stored in a retrieval
system, without written permission
obtained beforehand from
Search Press.

ISBN: 978-1-78221-172-3

The Publishers and author can
accept no responsibility for any
consequences arising from the
information, advice or instructions
given in this publication.

Suppliers
If you have difficulty in obtaining
any of the materials and equipment
mentioned in this book, then please
visit the Search Press website for
details of suppliers:
www.searchpress.com

Printed in China

General information

Types of canvas

Most canvases are made from cotton. However, silk is used to create very fine canvases and today, synthetic canvases can also be found. Canvases are available in a variety of gauges or counts and are assigned a number. This number describes the coarseness of the canvas. It is determined by counting the number of threads within a 2.5cm (1") distance, hence the larger the number attributed to a canvas, the finer it is.

Plain mono canvas

Plain mono canvas is created from individual warp and weft threads which are woven together in a basic over-under-over pattern. It is very strong but can be easily distorted if you stitch with a tension that is too firm.

Interlock mono canvas

Interlock mono canvas is not as strong as plain mono canvas but the weave cannot be distorted. Each single warp thread consists of two narrower threads that are twisted together and actually lock around the weft threads.

Double or 'Penelope' canvas

This durable canvas is woven with pairs of threads, which result in the formation of both large and small holes. Both sets of holes can be utilized for stitching. This is particularly beneficial for adding fine details to an embroidery.

Plastic canvas

Plastic canvas is moulded, rather than woven and is quite rigid. It can be used for projects such as boxes and bags.

Waste canvas

Waste canvas allows you to work needlepoint stitches onto plain fabrics and is designed to be removed. Position the canvas onto the right side of the plain fabric and tack in place. Work the embroidery with a sharp-pointed needle, taking care not to pierce the canvas threads. When the embroidery is complete, dampen the canvas to soften the threads and remove the threads with blunt-ended tweezers.

Rug canvas

This coarse canvas is generally made in a similar manner to interlock mono canvas.

Preparing canvas

Always be generous with the amount of canvas you allow for a project. For larger projects, cut canvas 10cm (4") longer and wider than the finished design area. Small designs don't require quite this much allowance.

Bind the edges of the canvas with masking tape. This prevents the canvas from pricking your fingers and the embroidery threads from snagging.

Berlin work

Threads

A vast array of threads and yarns can be used for canvas stitchery. The most important consideration, besides the colour and type, is the thickness. The selected threads should be thick enough so that the canvas does not peep through between the stitches.

If you are working a large area with the same thread, ensure that all skeins are of the same dyelot.

Test threads and stitches on a scrap of canvas before incorporating them into your design.

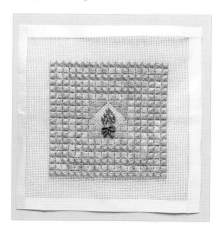

Stranded cotton

These low sheen threads come in an amazing variety of colours and are easy to work with. You can vary the thickness of the thread by altering the number of strands used. When using more than one strand at a time, it is important to separate the strands and then put them back together. This is known as 'stripping' the thread.

Perlé cotton

Perlé cotton is generally available in four different weights, or thicknesses – nos. 3, 5, 8 and 12. The larger the number, the finer the thread.

Silk thread

A wide range of silk threads, from flat untwisted filament silk to heavy twist buttonhole thread, is available. Silk adds an extra lustre, which appeals to many embroiderers.

Rayon thread

Rayon threads have a spectacular sheen, favoured by many embroiderers. They do have a mind of their own and can be difficult to use. Moisten the thread to make it easier to handle and use short lengths to minimise twisting and tangling.

Metallic thread

Metallic thread can be difficult to work with and can wear easily. Use short lengths of thread to make it more manageable.

Wool

Tapestry, crewel and rug wools are strong, durable yarns. In particular, tapestry and crewel wools come in an extensive colour range. These yarns are made with much longer fibres than yarn made for knitting and crochet and as a result are much stronger.

Tools

Needles

Tapestry needles are the most suitable for needlepoint. The large eye allows for easy threading and the blunt tip ensures they do not split the threads of the canvas. These needles are available in sizes 18 to 28 and the larger the number the finer the needle. However, you will find sizes 18 to 22 are the most commonly used. Select a needle that will easily pass through the holes in the canvas.

Scissors

Good quality, well maintained scissors make a huge difference to the ease and quality of your work. Two pairs of scissors are recommended for needlepoint. You will need a small pair with fine, sharp blades and tip for snipping threads and yarn. A larger, heavier pair is necessary for cutting canvas but avoid using your best fabric scissors. Because canvas is so tough, it will easily blunt them.

Needlepoint panel c1720

Hoops and frames

Small projects can be worked by holding the canvas freely in your hands. Larger pieces of needlepoint are likely to become distorted, in which case a frame is recommended while stitching. Both roller and slate frames are suitable for mounting canvas. A roller frame will allow you to scroll down the canvas as your design progresses. However, this can be a time consuming process as the sides will require relacing each time you reposition the length of canvas.

If your frame is much larger than the piece of canvas you wish to work on, attach panels of fabric to the sides before mounting it in the frame.

Many frames come with adjustable stands so you can alter the angle and height of the taut canvas to suit your comfort and stitching requirements.

Hoops are not a good option for canvaswork unless you are working on a very fine mesh fabric. Standard canvases are really too stiff to be adequately held in an embroidery hoop.

Masking tape

Use a 25mm (1") wide masking tape to bind the edges of the canvas. This will stop plain mono and 'Penelope' canvas from fraying and prevent interlock mono canvas from snagging threads.

Stiletto

A stiletto is valuable for separating canvas threads when working eyelets.

Starting, finishing and joining threads

Starting with a waste knot

Knot the end of the thread. Position the knot approximately 5cm (2") away from where the first stitch will be placed and in the path of the stitching. Take the needle from the front to the back so the knot shows on the right side of the canvas. Pull the thread through and then bring it to the front at the starting point for the first stitch.

As you stitch, the thread will be secured in the stitching on the back of the canvas. When you are near to the waste knot, cut it off close to the canvas.

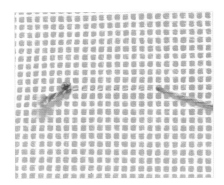

Ending off

Take the needle to the back of the canvas. Weave it backwards and forwards through several stitches and then trim the tail. If required, add a back stitch for extra security.

Joining in a new thread

Weave the new thread backwards and forwards through several stitches on the back of the canvas near where you wish to begin stitching. Bring the thread to the front and begin stitching. Alternatively, the waste knot method can be used.

Blocking

It is worth blocking your needlepoint even if it has been worked in a frame. The process restiffens the canvas, ensures it is square and freshens the stitching.

Place the embroidered piece face down on an ironing board and cover with a damp towel. Steam press to dampen the needlepoint.

Pin the pattern or grid paper to a blocking board and cover with greaseproof paper, heavy tracing paper or plastic film. Pin in place. Position the damp needlepoint, face down, onto the pattern or grid paper. Stretch and pin the needlepoint to the board, ensuring the centre and sides are aligned. Leave in place until completely dry.

If the canvas is badly distorted, thoroughly dampen it by rolling it in a wet towel or sponging it. Ensure the moisture penetrates both the canvas and the stitches. Stretch the canvas in the opposite direction to the distortion by pulling on opposite corners and then pulling opposite sides. Pin to the blocking board in the same manner as before.

Needlepoint trunk

Hints for stitching

- When working each stitch, bring the thread to the front through an empty hole wherever possible. Take the thread to the back by going down a hole that already has a stitch or stitches in it. This method eliminates 'fluffy' stitches on the right side of the canvas.

- Correct tension is important. The stitches should lie snugly against the canvas but not be so tight that they distort the weave.

- When stitching a pattern, work as many complete stitches as possible first. Work part stitches in any remaining spaces around the outer edge of the section.

Georgian needlepoint sofa

Needlepoint stitches

ALGERIAN EYE STITCH

Also known as star eyelet stitch.

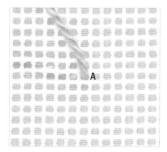

1 Secure the thread on the upper left hand side. Bring it to the front at A, one canvas thread above and to the left of the centre hole.

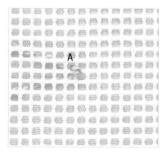

2 Take the needle to the back through the centre hole. Pull the thread through.

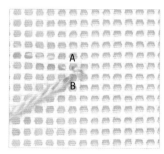

3 Re-emerge at B, one canvas thread to the left of the centre hole. Pull the thread through.

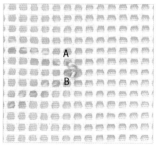

4 Again, take the needle to the back through the centre hole. Pull the thread through.

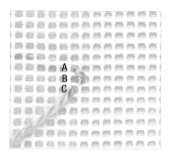

5 Re-emerge at C, one canvas thread below B. Pull the thread through.

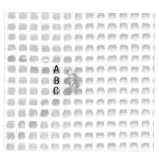

6 Again, take the needle to the back through the centre hole. Pull the thread through.

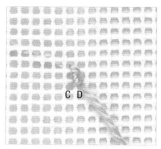

7 Re-emerge at D, one canvas thread to the right of C. Pull the thread through.

8 Again, take the needle to the back through the centre hole. Pull the thread through.

9 Re-emerge at E, one canvas thread to the right of D. Pull the thread through.

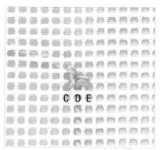

10 Again, take the needle to the back through the centre hole. Pull the thread through.

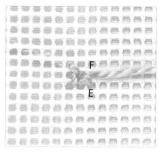

11 Re-emerge at F, one canvas thread above E. Pull the thread through.

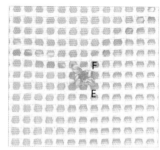

12 Again, take the needle to the back through the centre hole. Pull the thread through.

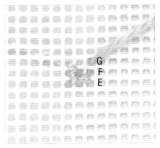

13 Re-emerge at G, one canvas thread above F. Pull the thread through.

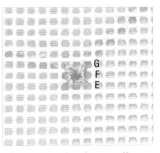

14 Again, take the needle to the back through the centre hole. Pull the thread through.

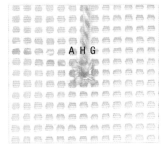

15 Re-emerge at H, one canvas thread to the left of G. Pull the thread through.

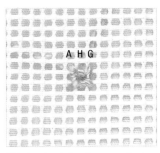

16 Again, take the needle to the back through the centre hole. Pull the thread through.

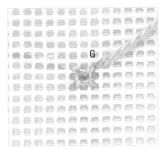

17 To begin the second stitch, bring the needle to the front at G. Pull the thread through.

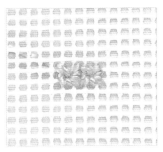

18 Work the second stitch, following steps 2–16. Take care not to split the thread in the shared holes on the left hand side.

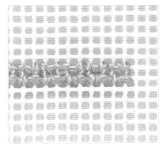

19 Continue working stitches across the row in the same manner.

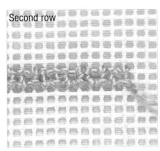

20 Bring the needle to the front through the same hole as the lower right hand corner of the last stitch.

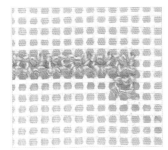

21 Working clockwise rather than anticlockwise, work the stitch in the same manner as before. Take care not to split the thread in the shared holes on the upper side.

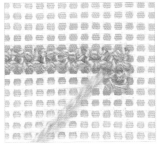

22 To begin the second stitch of this row, bring the needle to the front through the same hole as the upper left hand corner of the previous stitch. Pull the thread through.

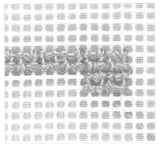

23 Complete the stitch in the same manner as before.

24 Continue working rows of stitches back and forth across the canvas. When working from left to right, work the stitches anticlockwise. When working from right to left, work the stitches clockwise.

AUBUSSON STITCH

Also known as rep stitch, this stitch must be worked on double-thread or Penelope canvas.

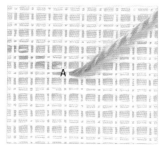

1 Secure the thread on the upper left hand side. Bring it to the front at A, between the pair of threads on the left hand side of an intersection.

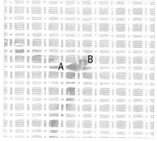

2 Take the needle to the back at B, in the upper right hand corner of the intersection. Pull the thread through.

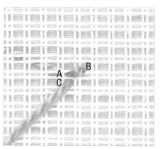

3 Re-emerge at C, in the lower left hand corner of the intersection. Pull the thread through.

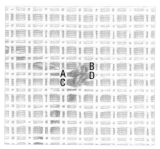

4 Take the needle to the back at D, between the pair of threads on the right hand side of the intersection. Pull the thread through.

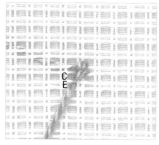

5 To begin the second stitch, bring the needle to the front at E, one thread directly below C. Pull the thread through.

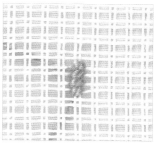

6 Work the second stitch following steps 2–4.

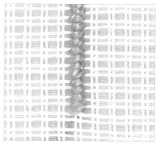

7 Continue working stitches downwards in the same manner.

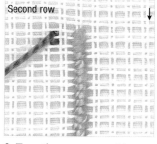

8 Turn the canvas upside down. Bring the thread to the front between the pair of threads one intersection to the left of the first row.

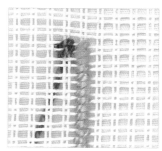

9 Work the stitch following steps 2–4. Take care not to split the thread in the shared holes.

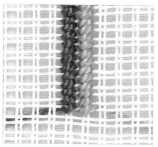

10 Complete the row in the same manner as before.

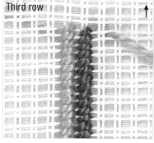

11 Turn the canvas upside down. Bring the thread to the front between the pair of threads one intersection to the right of the second row.

12 Complete the row as before. Continue working rows of stitches in the same manner, turning the canvas after each one.

Some history

Canvaswork has its roots in ancient times. Needlepoint, dating back to 1500BC, has been discovered in the tomb of an Egyptian Pharaoh. It has also appeared in the writings of Imperial Rome where it was used to create couch cushions. Coptic work in 4th–5th century AD often used tent or cross stitch on linen.

During the Middle Ages, canvaswork was called opus pulvinarium, which meant 'cushionwork'. It was used for kneeling mats, cushions and the like in the churches and abbeys. It was stitched on coarsely-woven linen fabric which was similar to canvas mesh. Steel needles were also invented around this time and this allowed embroiderers to create more intricate work than they had been able to with the fishbone or thorn needles used previously.

One of the most famous of all embroiderers lived in the 16th century – Mary, Queen of Scots. Mary had grown up in the French court where she studied embroidery extensively. As a rival of Queen Elizabeth I, she spent many years of her life imprisoned. To pass the time, among other projects, she stitched an enormous number of tent stitch emblems bordered with metal thread. These emblems were cut out and applied to bed curtains, coverlets, hangings and cushions.

BACK STITCH

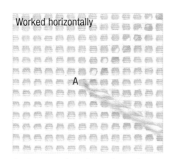

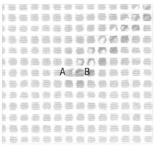

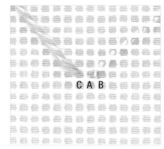

1 Secure the thread on the right hand side. Bring it to the front at A, just to the left of the first canvas thread to be covered.

2 Take the needle to the back at B, on the right hand side of the canvas thread. Pull the thread through.

3 To begin the second stitch, re-emerge at C, on the left hand side of the next canvas thread to the left. Pull the thread through.

4 Take the needle to the back at A, taking care not to split the thread of the previous stitch. Pull the thread through.

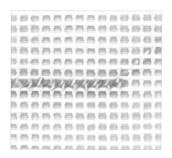

5 Continue working stitches across the row in the same manner.

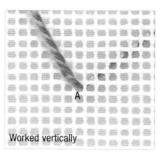

Worked vertically

1 Secure the thread near the top. Bring it to the front at A, just below the first canvas thread to be covered.

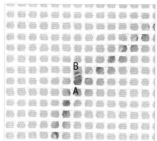

2 Take the needle to the back at B, just above the canvas thread. Pull the thread through.

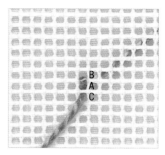

3 To begin the second stitch, re-emerge at C, below the next canvas thread. Pull the thread through.

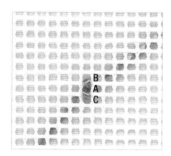

4 Take the needle to the back at A, taking care not to split the thread of the previous stitch. Pull the thread through.

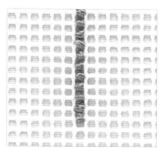

5 Continue working stitches down the row in the same manner.

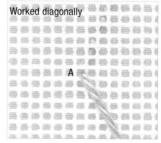

Worked diagonally

1 Secure the thread near the top. Bring it to the front at A, just below the first intersection to be covered.

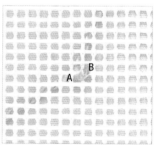

2 Take the needle over the intersection and to the back at B, diagonally opposite. Pull the thread through.

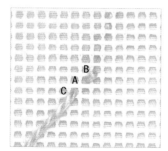

3 To begin the second stitch, re-emerge at C, below the next intersection. Pull the thread through.

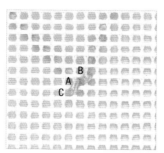

4 Take the needle to the back at A, taking care not to split the thread of the previous stitch. Pull the thread through.

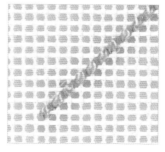

5 Continue working stitches along the row in the same manner.

BACK STITCHED SPIDER WEB

1 To form the foundation, work an Algerian eye stitch following the instructions on pages 10–11.

2 Bring the needle to the front one canvas thread below the centre hole of the Algerian eye and to the right of the vertical spoke.

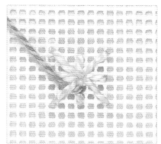

3 Pull the thread through. Working in a clockwise direction, weave the thread over the vertical spoke and under the next spoke.

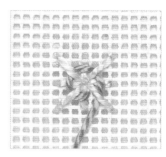

4 Continue weaving over and under until reaching the first spoke.

5 Pull the thread firmly.

6 Take the needle, from right to left, under the last spoke and then the first spoke.

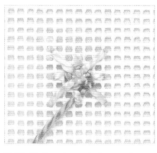

7 Pull the thread through until it wraps snugly around the spoke but does not distort it.

8 Take the needle, from right to left, under the first spoke and then the second spoke.

9 Pull the thread through as before.

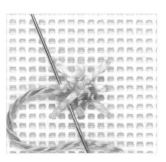

10 Take the needle under the second spoke and then the third spoke.

11 Pull the thread through as before. Continue working stitches in the same manner, spiralling out from the centre, until the spokes are completely covered.

12 To finish, take the needle to the back of the canvas just over the last used spoke.

BASKETWEAVE STITCH

Basketweave stitch is a tent stitch worked diagonally across the canvas.

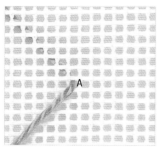

1 Secure the thread on the upper left hand side. Bring it to the front at A, the base of the stitch.

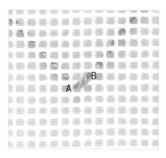

2 Crossing one intersection, take the needle to the back at B, diagonally above and to the right. Pull the thread through.

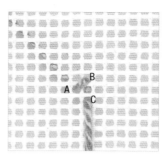

3 To begin the second stitch, bring the needle to the front at C, two canvas threads below B. Pull the thread through.

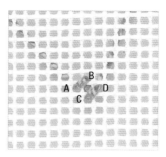

4 Crossing one intersection, take the needle to the back at D, diagonally above and to the right. Pull the thread through.

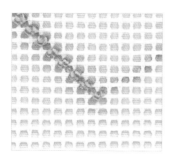

5 Continue working downwards in the same manner to the end of the row.

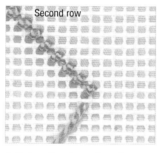

6 Bring the thread to the front one canvas thread below the lower end of the last stitch.

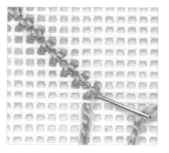

7 Take the needle to the back through the hole diagonally above and to the right.

8 Pull the thread through. To begin the second stitch of this row, re-emerge through the second hole to the left.

9 Take the needle to the back through the hole diagonally above and to the right.

10 Continue working upwards in the same manner to the end of the row.

11 Continue working rows of stitches diagonally up and down the canvas.

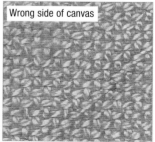

12 On the back of the canvas, a basketweave design appears.

BRICK STITCH

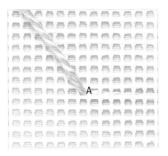

1 Secure the thread on the upper right hand side. Bring it to the front at A, the base of the stitch.

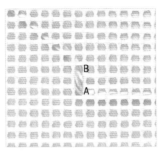

2 Crossing two canvas threads, take the needle to the back at B, directly above. Pull the thread through.

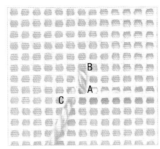

3 To begin the second stitch, bring the thread to the front at C, one canvas thread to the left and three canvas threads below B.

4 Crossing two canvas threads, take the needle to the back at D, directly above. Pull the thread through.

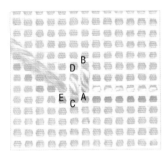

5 To begin the third stitch, bring the thread to the front at E, crossing one intersection.

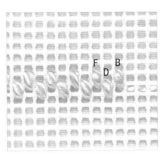

6 Crossing two canvas threads, take the needle to the back at F, directly above. Pull the thread through. Continue working stitches across the row in the same manner.

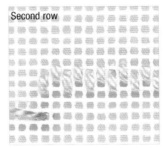

7 Bring the thread to the front two canvas threads directly below the last stitch.

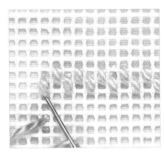

8 Take the needle to the back through the same hole as the base of the previous stitch. Take care not to split the previous stitch.

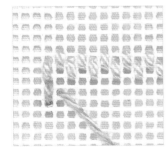

9 Pull the thread through. Re-emerge two canvas threads directly below the second to last stitch of the previous row.

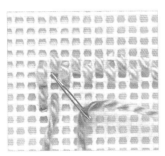

10 Take the needle to the back through the same hole as the base of the stitch directly above. Take care not to split the stitch.

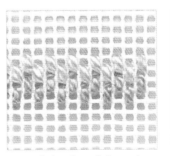

11 Pull the thread through. Continue across the row in the same manner.

12 Continue working rows of stitches, back and forth, across the canvas in the same manner.

BRIGHTON STITCH

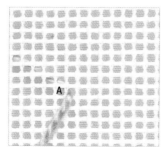

1 Secure the thread on the upper left hand side. Bring it to the front at A, on the left hand side of the stitch.

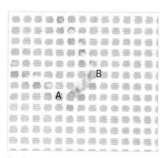

2 Crossing two intersections, take the needle to the back at B, diagonally above and to the right. Pull the thread through.

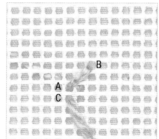

3 Re-emerge at C, one canvas thread below A. Pull the thread through.

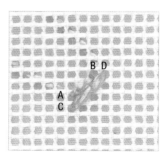

4 Take the needle to the back at D, one canvas thread to the right of B. Pull the thread through.

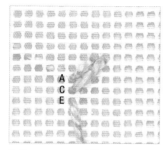

5 Re-emerge at E, one canvas thread below C. Pull the thread through.

6 Take the needle to the back at F, one canvas thread to the right of D. Pull the thread through.

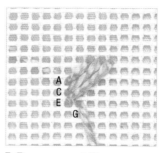

7 Re-emerge at G, one canvas thread to the right of E. Pull the thread through.

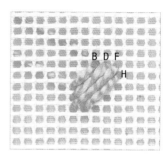

8 Take the needle to the back at H, one canvas thread below F. Pull the thread through.

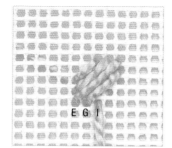

9 Re-emerge at I, one canvas thread to the right of G. Pull the thread through.

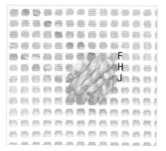

10 Take the needle to the back at J, one canvas thread below H. Pull the thread through.

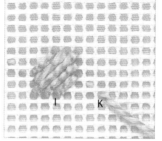

11 Re-emerge at K, four canvas threads to the right of I. Pull the thread through.

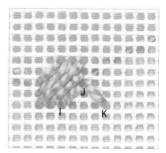

12 Take the needle to the back at J, taking care not to split the thread that shares the hole. Pull the thread through.

↑ Indicates top of canvas

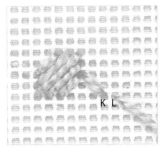

13 Re-emerge at L, one canvas thread to the right of K. Pull the thread through.

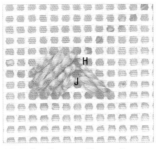

14 Take the needle to the back at H, taking care not to split the thread that shares the hole. Pull the thread through.

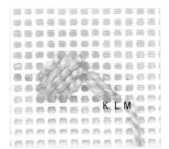

15 Re-emerge at M, one canvas thread to the right of L. Pull the thread through.

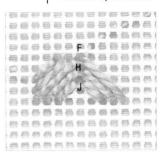

16 Take the needle to the back at F, taking care not to split the thread that shares the hole. Pull the thread through.

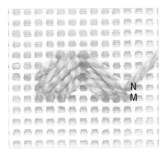

17 Re-emerge at N, one canvas thread above M. Pull the thread through.

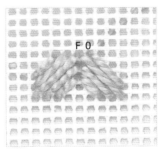

18 Take the needle to the back at O, one canvas thread to the right of F. Pull the thread through.

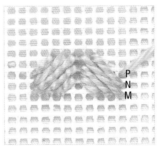

19 Re-emerge at P, one canvas thread above N. Pull the thread through.

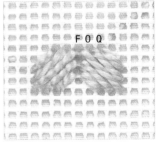

20 Take the needle to the back at Q, one canvas thread to the right of O. Pull the thread through.

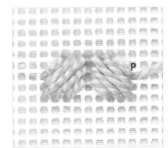

21 To start the sequence of diagonal stitches again, bring the thread to the front at P, taking care not to split the thread that shares the hole. Pull the thread through.

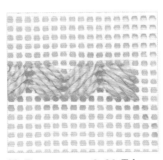

22 Repeat steps 2–20. Take care not to split the thread in the shared holes.

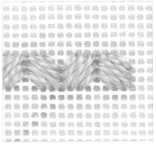

23 Working from left to right, continue working stitches across the row.

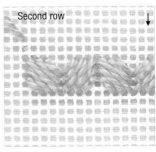

24 Turn the canvas upside down. Bring the thread to the front two canvas threads above the top left hand corner of the previous row.

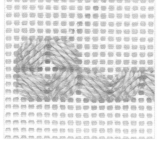

25 Working from left to right, begin working stitches across the row in the same manner as before. Take care not to split the thread in the shared holes.

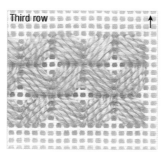

26 Complete the row. Turn the canvas upside down. Work the third row in the same manner as the first row.

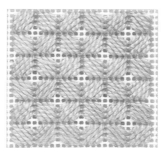

27 Continue working the desired number of rows, turning the canvas after each one.

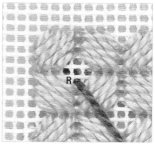

28 Using a new thread, bring it to the front at R, one canvas thread below the centre of the first diamond-shaped space.

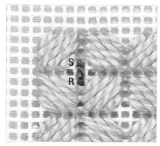

29 Crossing two canvas threads, take the needle to the back at S, above. Pull the thread through.

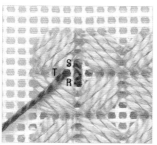

30 Re-emerge at T, halfway between R and S and one canvas thread to the left. Pull the thread through.

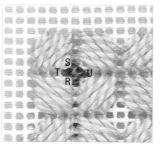

31 Crossing two canvas threads, take the needle to the back at U, on the right hand side. Pull the thread through to complete an upright cross stitch.

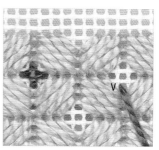

32 Carrying the thread on the back, bring it to the front at V, in the next diamond-shaped space.

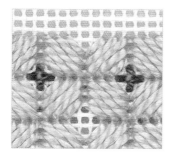

33 Work a second upright cross stitch, following steps 29–31.

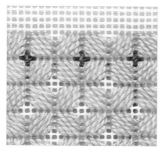

34 Working from left to right, continue across the row in the same manner.

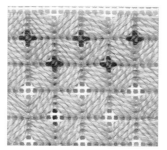

35 Work the second row of upright cross stitches from right to left.

36 Continue working rows of stitches, back and forth, across the canvas.

BYZANTINE STITCH

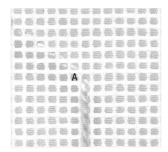

1 Secure the thread on the upper left hand side. Bring it to the front at A.

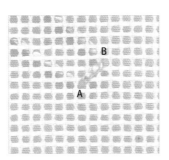

2 Crossing two canvas intersections, take the needle to the back at B, diagonally above and to the right. Pull the thread through.

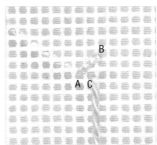

3 Re-emerge at C, one canvas thread to the right of A. Pull the thread through.

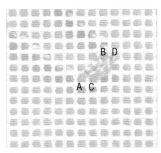

4 Take the needle to the back at D, one canvas thread to the right of B. Pull the thread through.

5 Stitching from left to right, work two more diagonal stitches in exactly the same manner.

6 Bring the thread to the front, one canvas thread below the base of the previous stitch.

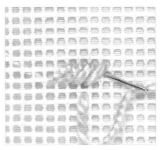

7 Take the needle to the back, one canvas thread below the tip of the previous stitch.

8 Pull the thread through. Stitching downwards, work two more diagonal stitches in exactly the same manner.

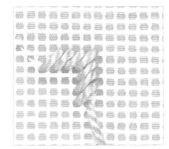

9 Bring the thread to the front, one canvas thread to the right of the base of the previous stitch.

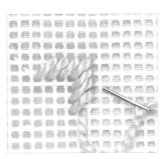

10 Take the needle to the back, one canvas thread to the right of the tip of the previous stitch.

11 Pull the thread through. Stitching from left to right, work two more diagonal stitches in exactly the same manner.

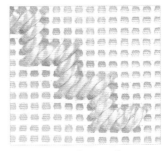

12 Working diagonally from left to right, continue working stitches across the row.

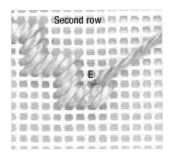

13 Bring the thread to the front through the same hole as the tip of the third to last stitch of the previous row (E).

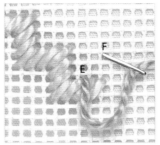

14 Crossing two canvas intersections, take the needle to the back at F, diagonally upwards and to the right.

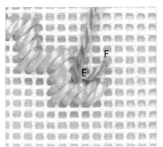

15 Pull the thread through. Re-emerge one canvas thread to the left of E. Pull the thread through.

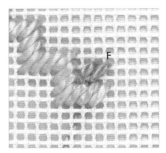

16 Take the needle to the back one canvas thread to the left of F. Pull the thread through.

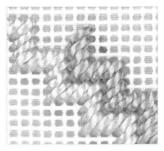

17 Working diagonally from right to left, continue working stitches across the row. Ensure the base of each new stitch shares a hole with a stitch of the previous row.

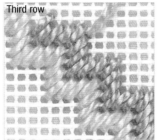

18 Bring the thread to the front through the same hole as the closest stitch to the left hand side which is two intersections below the top of the stitching.

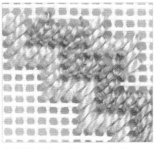

19 Working diagonally from left to right, continue working stitches across the row. Take care not to split the thread in the shared holes.

20 Continue working rows of stitches, back and forth, across the canvas.

Linen and hemp

During the Middle Ages, linen and hempen cloth were used as a ground for needlepoint. Linen was produced from the flax plant and hempen cloth was a product of the cannabis plant, along with rope, oil, sailcloth and tents. While much has been made of linen, it appears to have been rivalled by hemp.

"Hemp grows in the country of the Scythians, which except in the thickness and height of the stalk, very much resembles flax; in the qualities mentioned, however, the hemp is much superior. The Thracians make clothing of it very like linen; nor could any person without being very well acquainted with the substance, say whether this clothing be made of hemp or flax."

Herodotus

flax

CASHMERE STITCH

1 Secure the thread on the upper right hand side. Bring it to the front at A, the base of the stitch.

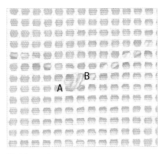

2 Crossing one canvas intersection, take the needle to the back at B, above and to the right. Pull the thread through.

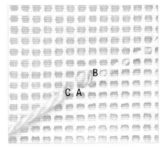

3 Re-emerge at C, one canvas thread to the left of A. Pull the thread through.

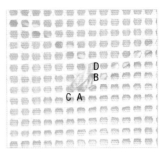

4 Take the needle to the back at D, one canvas thread above B. Pull the thread through.

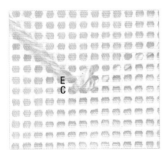

5 Re-emerge at E, one canvas thread above C. Pull the thread through.

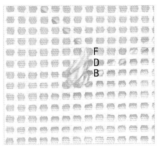

6 Take the needle to the back at F, one canvas thread above D. Pull the thread through.

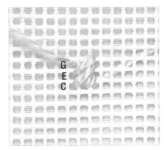

7 Re-emerge at G, one canvas thread above E. Pull the thread through.

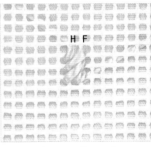

8 Take the needle to the back at H, one canvas thread to the left of F. Pull the thread through.

9 To begin the second cashmere stitch, bring the thread to the front one canvas thread to the left of C. Pull the thread through.

10 Work the second stitch following steps 2–8. Take care not to split the thread in the shared holes.

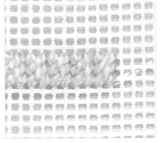

11 Working from right to left, continue working stitches across the row.

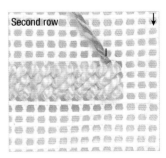

12 Turn the canvas upside down. Bring the thread to the front at I.

23

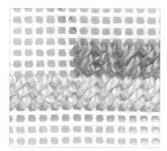

13 Continue working rows of stitches in the same manner, turning the canvas after each one.

14 Working from right to left, work stitches across the row in the same manner as the first row. Take care not to split the thread in the shared holes.

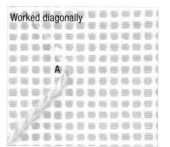

Worked diagonally

1 Secure the thread on the upper left hand side. Bring it to the front at A.

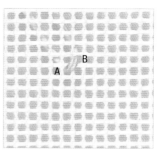

2 Crossing one canvas intersection, take the needle to the back at B, above and to the right. Pull the thread through.

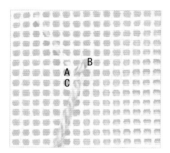

3 Re-emerge at C, one canvas thread below A. Pull the thread through.

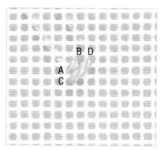

4 Take the needle to the back at D, one canvas thread to the right of B. Pull the thread through.

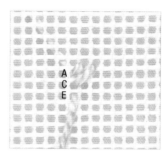

5 Re-emerge at E, one canvas thread below C. Pull the thread through.

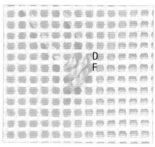

6 Take the needle to the back at F, one canvas thread below D. Pull the thread through.

7 Re-emerge at G, one canvas thread to the right of E. Pull the thread through.

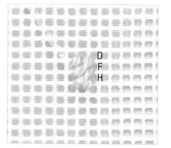

8 Take the needle to the back at H, one canvas thread below F. Pull the thread through.

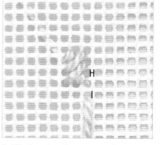

9 To begin the second cashmere stitch, bring the thread to the front at I, two canvas threads below H. Pull the thread through.

10 Work the second stitch following steps 2–8.

24

11 Working diagonally from left to right, continue working stitches across the row.

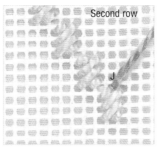

12 Bring the needle to the front at J, sharing the hole at the top of the previous stitch.

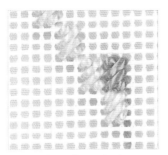

13 Working from the bottom upwards, work the first stitch in a similar manner to those of the first row. Take care not to split the thread in the shared holes.

14 Working from right to left, work stitches across the row in the same manner. Take care not to split the thread in the shared holes.

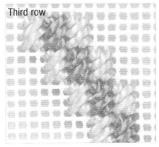

15 Stitch the third row in exactly the same manner as the first row. Take care not to split the thread in the shared holes.

16 Continue working rows of stitches, back and forth, across the canvas.

A word about terminology

The term needlepoint is often used to describe canvaswork that relies heavily on tent stitch. Petit point refers to very fine work and gros point to coarse work. Needlepoint is often mistakenly called tapestry, a term that is frequently misused.

True tapestries are formed by weaving and were often used as wall hangings and rugs in the great houses of medieval Europe. During the 16th and 17th centuries, needlepoint was used to create these wall hangings and rugs, and so the terms became confused.

CHEQUER STITCH

Chequer stitch is a combination of Scottish stitch and basketweave tent stitches.

1 Secure the thread on the upper right hand side. Work a Scottish stitch following steps 1–10 on page 105.

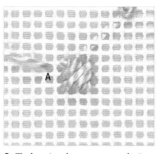

2 To begin the square of nine tent stitches, bring the needle to the front at A, one canvas thread to the left of the base of the previous stitch. Pull the thread through.

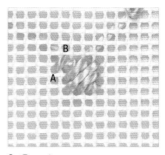

3 Crossing one canvas intersection, take the needle to the back at B, above and to the right. Pull the thread through.

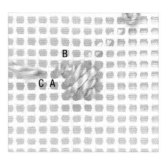

4 Re-emerge at C, one canvas thread to the left of A. Pull the thread through.

5 Crossing one canvas intersection, take the needle to the back at D, above and to the right. Pull the thread through.

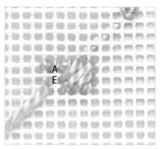

6 Re-emerge at E, one canvas thread below A. Pull the thread through.

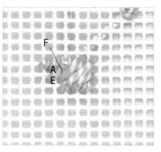

7 Crossing one canvas intersection, take the needle to the back at F, above and to the right. Pull the thread through.

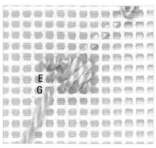

8 Re-emerge at G, one canvas thread below E. Pull the thread through.

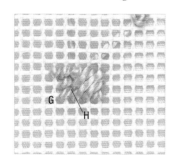

9 Crossing one canvas intersection, take the needle to the back at H, above and to the right. Pull the thread through.

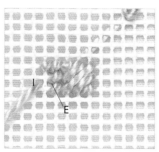

10 Re-emerge at I, one canvas thread to the left of E. Pull the thread through.

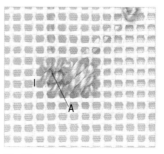

11 Crossing one canvas intersection, take the needle to the back at A, above and to the right. Pull the thread through.

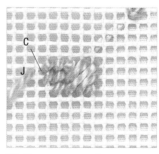

12 Re-emerge at J, one canvas thread to the left of C. Pull the thread through.

↑ Indicates top of canvas

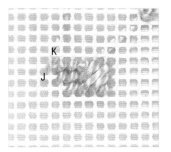

13 Crossing one canvas intersection, take the needle to the back at K, above and to the right. Pull the thread through.

14 Re-emerge at L, one canvas thread to the left of I. Pull the thread through.

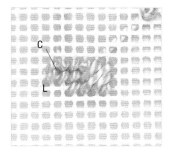

15 Crossing one canvas intersection, take the needle to the back at C, above and to the right. Pull the thread through.

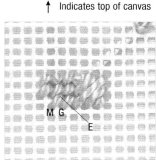

16 Re-emerge at M, one canvas thread to the left of G. Take the needle to the back at E, above and to the right. Pull the thread through.

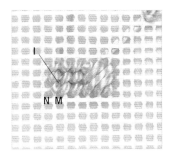

17 Re-emerge at N, one canvas thread to the left of M. Take the needle to the back at I. Pull the thread through.

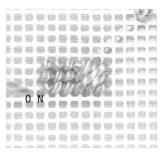

18 To begin the second Scottish stitch, bring the needle to the front at O, one canvas thread to the left of N. Pull the thread through.

19 Work the second Scottish stitch in the same manner as before.

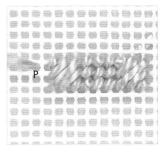

20 To begin the second square of tent stitches bring the needle to the front at P, one canvas thread to the left of the base of the previous stitch. Pull the thread through.

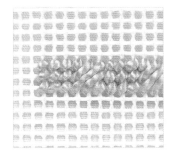

21 Working from right to left, continue across the row, alternating between a Scottish stitch and a square of nine tent stitches.

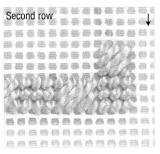

22 Turn the canvas upside down. Working in the same manner as before and above the first row, stitch the alternative square to the previous square.

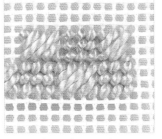

23 Working from right to left, continue across the row. Ensure the Scottish stitches and square of tent stitches alternate with the previous row as well as in this row.

24 Continue working rows of stitches in the same manner, turning the canvas after each one.

CONTINENTAL STITCH

Continental stitch is also known as tent stitch.

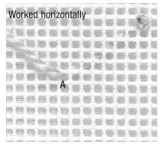

1 Secure the thread on the upper right hand side. Bring it to the front at A, the base of the stitch.

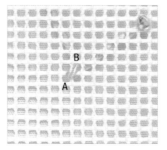

2 Crossing one canvas intersection, take the needle to the back at B, above and to the right. Pull the thread through.

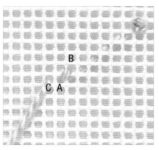

3 To begin the second stitch, bring the needle to the front at C, one canvas thread to the left of A. Pull the thread through.

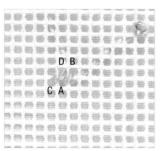

4 Crossing one canvas intersection, take the needle to the back at D, above and to the right. Pull the thread through.

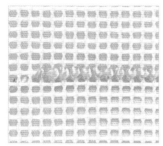

5 Working from right to left, continue working stitches across the row in the same manner.

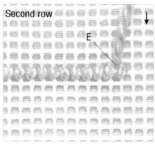

6 Turn the canvas upside down. Bring the needle to the front at E, through the same hole as the tip of the second to last stitch.

7 Work the stitch following step 2.

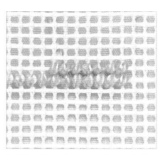

8 Working from right to left, work stitches across the row in the same manner. Take care not to split the thread in the shared holes.

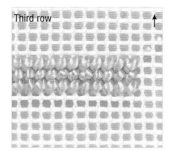

9 Turn the canvas upside down and stitch the third row in exactly the same manner as the first row.

10 Continue working rows of stitches in the same manner, turning the canvas after each one.

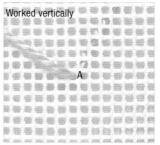

1 Secure the thread on the upper right hand side. Bring it to the front at A, the base of the stitch.

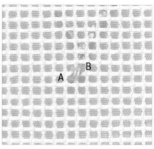

2 Crossing one canvas intersection, take the needle to the back at B, above and to the right. Pull the thread through.

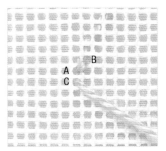

3 Re-emerge at C, one canvas thread directly below A. Pull the thread through.

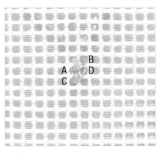

4 Crossing one canvas intersection, take the needle to the back at D, above and to the right. Pull the thread through.

5 Working downwards, continue working stitches to the end of the row in the same manner.

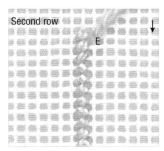

6 Turn the canvas upside down. Bring the thread to the front at E, through the same hole as the tip of the second to last stitch.

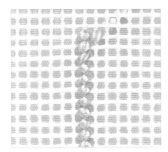

7 Work the stitch following step 2.

8 Working downwards, work stitches to the end of the row in the same manner. Take care not to split the thread in the shared holes.

Tent stitch

The word 'tent' is derived from the English word 'tenture' or 'tenter' (tendere – to stretch) referring to the frame that the linen was stretched on to work stitches.

Tent stitch is used in making and mending tents when they are made by hand and it is also found in the embroidered flaps of Arab tents.

9 Turn the canvas upside down and stitch the third row in exactly the same manner.

10 Continue working rows of stitches in the same manner, turning the canvas after each one.

Tent stitch picture, c1660

CROSS STITCH

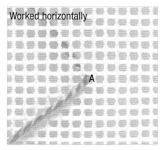

1 Secure the thread on the upper left hand side. Bring it to the front at A, the base of the stitch.

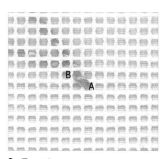

2 Crossing one canvas intersection, take the needle to the back at B, above and to the left. Pull the thread through.

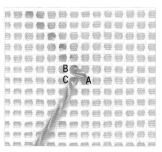

3 Re-emerge at C, one canvas thread directly below B. Pull the thread through.

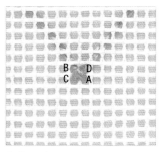

4 Crossing one canvas intersection, take the needle to the back at D, above and to the right. Pull the thread through.

5 To begin the second stitch, bring the thread to the front one canvas thread to the right of A. Pull the thread through.

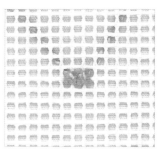

6 Work the second stitch following steps 2–4. Take care not to split the thread in the shared holes on the left hand side.

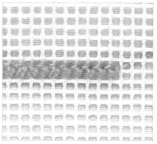

7 Working from left to right, continue working stitches across the row.

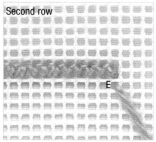

8 Bring the thread to the front at E, one canvas thread directly below the lower right corner of the previous stitch.

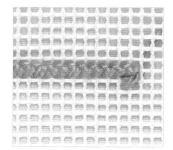

9 Work the stitch following steps 2–4. Take care not to split the thread in the shared holes.

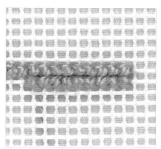

10 Working from right to left, work stitches across the row in the same manner. Take care not to split the thread in the shared holes.

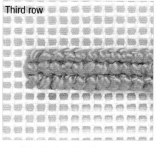

11 Stitch the third row in exactly the same manner as the first row.

12 Continue working rows of stitches, back and forth, across the canvas.

↑ Indicates top of canvas

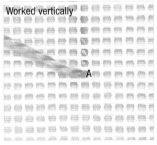

1 Secure the thread on the upper right hand side. Bring it to the front at A, the base of the stitch.

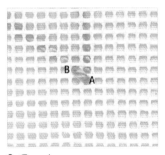

2 Crossing one canvas intersection, take the needle to the back at B, above and to the left. Pull the thread through.

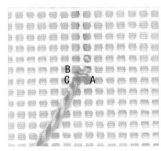

3 Re-emerge at C, one canvas thread directly below B. Pull the thread through.

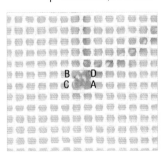

4 Crossing one canvas intersection, take the needle to the back at D, above and to the right. Pull the thread through.

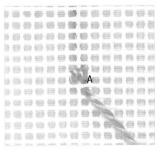

5 To begin the second stitch, bring the thread to the front one canvas thread below A. Pull the thread through.

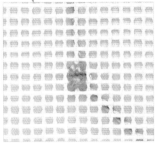

6 Work the second stitch following steps 2–4. Take care not to split the thread in the shared holes.

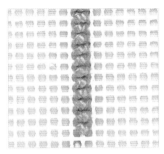

7 Working downwards, continue working stitches to the end of the row.

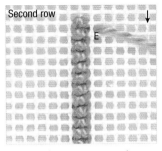

8 Turn the canvas upside down. Bring the thread to the front at E, one canvas thread to the right of the lower right corner of the previous stitch.

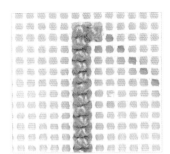

9 Work the stitch following steps 2–4. Take care not to split the thread in the shared holes.

10 Working downwards, continue working stitches to the end of the row. Take care not to split the thread in the shared holes.

11 Turn the canvas upside down and stitch the third row in exactly the same manner.

12 Continue working rows of stitches in the same manner, turning the canvas after each one.

CROSS STITCH – DOUBLE

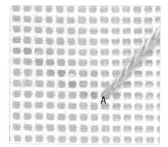

1 Secure the thread on the upper left hand side. Bring it to the front at A, the base of the stitch.

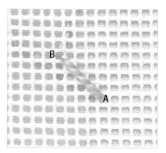

2 Crossing four canvas intersections, take the needle to the back at B, above and to the left. Pull the thread through.

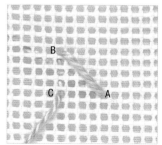

3 Re-emerge at C, four canvas threads directly below B. Pull the thread through.

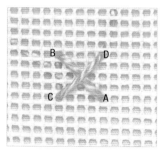

4 Crossing four canvas intersections, take the needle to the back at D, above and to the right. Pull the thread through.

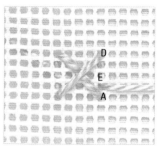

5 Re-emerge at E, three canvas threads directly below D. Pull the thread through.

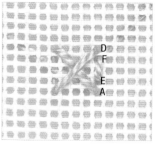

6 Take the needle to the back at F, two canvas threads above. Pull the thread through.

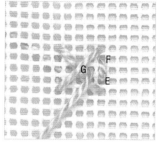

7 Re-emerge at G, one canvas intersection below and to the left. Pull the thread through.

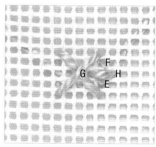

8 Take the needle to the back at H, two canvas threads to the right. Pull the thread through.

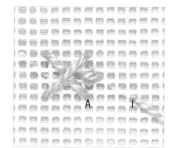

9 To begin the second sequence, bring the thread to the front at I, four canvas threads to the right of A. Pull the thread through.

10 Work the second sequence following steps 2–8. Take care not to split the thread in the shared holes on the left hand side.

11 Working from left to right, continue working stitches across the row.

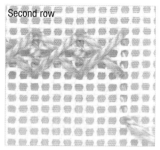

12 Bring the thread to the front four canvas threads directly below the lower right corner of the previous stitch.

↑ Indicates top of canvas

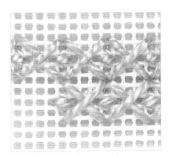

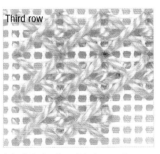

13 Working from right to left, work stitches across the row in the same manner.

14 Stitch the third row in exactly the same manner as the first row.

15 Continue working rows of stitches back and forth across the canvas.

16 If desired, work upright cross stitches in the diamond shapes between the rows.

CROSS STITCH – HALF

Also known as tent stitch, it is best worked on double or Penelope canvas.

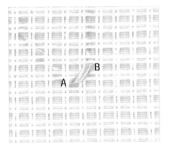

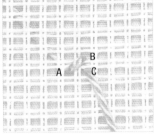

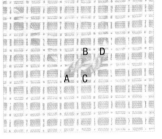

1 Secure the thread on the upper left hand side. Bring it to the front at A, the base of the stitch.

2 Crossing one canvas intersection, take the needle to the back at B, above and to the right. Pull the thread through.

3 To begin the second stitch, bring the needle to the front at C, one pair of canvas threads directly below B. Pull the thread through.

4 Crossing one canvas intersection, take the needle to the back at D, above and to the right. Pull the thread through.

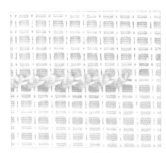

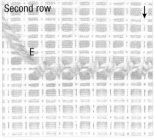

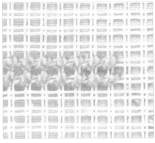

5 Working from left to right, continue working stitches across the row in the same manner.

6 Turn the canvas upside down. Bring the thread to the front at E, one pair of canvas threads directly above the end of the previous stitch.

7 Work the stitch following step 2.

8 Working from left to right, work stitches across the row in the same manner. Take care not to split the thread in the shared holes.

CROSS STITCH – HALF / CONTINUED

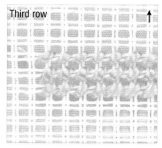

9 Turn the canvas upside down and stitch the third row in exactly the same manner as the first row. Take care not to split the thread in the shared holes.

10 Continue working rows of stitches in the same manner, turning the canvas after each one.

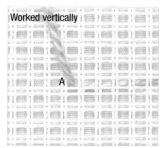

1 Secure the thread on the lower right hand side. Bring it to the front at A, the base of the stitch.

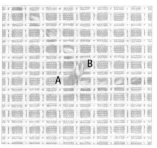

2 Crossing one canvas intersection, take the needle to the back at B, above and to the right. Pull the thread through.

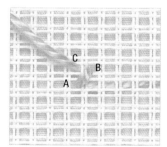

3 Re-emerge at C, one pair of canvas threads directly above A. Pull the thread through.

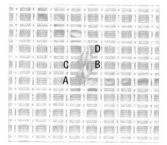

4 Crossing one canvas intersection, take the needle to the back at D, above and to the right. Pull the thread through.

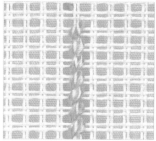

5 Working upwards, continue working stitches to the end of the row in the same manner.

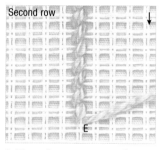

6 Turn the canvas upside down. Bring the thread to the front at E, one pair of canvas threads to the right of the base of the previous stitch.

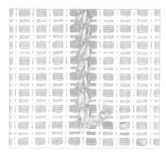

7 Work the stitch following step 2.

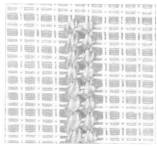

8 Working upwards, work stitches to the end of the row in the same manner. Take care not to split the thread in the shared holes.

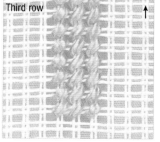

9 Turn the canvas upside down and stitch the third row in exactly the same manner as the first row.

10 Continue working rows of stitches in the same manner, turning the canvas after each one.

CROSS STITCH – LONG-ARMED

Long-armed cross stitch is also known as long-legged stitch, plaited Slav stitch, Portuguese stitch and twist stitch.

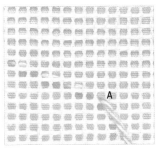

1 Secure the thread on the upper left hand side. Bring it to the front at A, the base of the stitch.

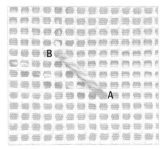

2 Crossing four canvas intersections, take the needle to the back at B, above and to the left. Pull the thread through.

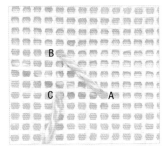

3 Re-emerge at C, four canvas threads below B. Pull the thread through.

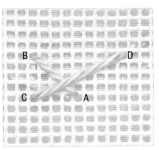

4 Take the needle to the back at D, eight canvas threads to the right of B. Pull the thread through.

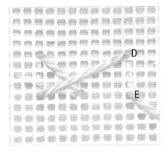

5 To begin the second stitch, bring the thread to the front at E, four canvas threads below D. Pull the thread through.

6 Work the second stitch following steps 2–4.

7 Working from left to right, continue working stitches across the row.

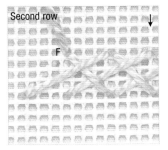

8 Turn the canvas upside down. Bring the thread to the front at F, through the same hole as the tip of the short arm of the previous stitch.

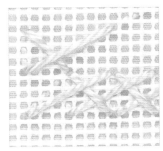

9 Work the stitch following steps 2–4. Take care not to split the thread in the shared holes.

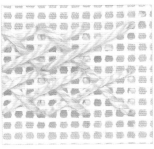

10 Working from left to right, work stitches across the row in the same manner. Take care not to split the thread in the shared holes.

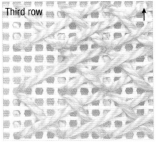

11 Turn the canvas upside down. Stitch the third row in exactly the same manner as the first row.

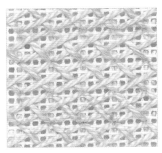

12 Continue working rows of stitches in the same manner, turning the canvas after each one.

35

CROSS STITCH – MONTENEGRIN

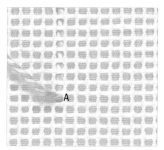

1 Secure the thread on the upper left hand side. Bring it to the front at A, the base of the stitch.

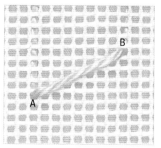

2 Take the needle to the back at B, four canvas threads above and eight canvas threads to the right. Pull the thread through.

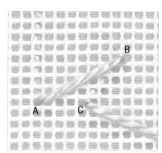

3 Re-emerge at C, four canvas threads to the right of A. Pull the thread through.

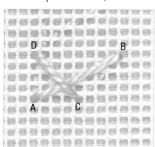

4 Take the needle to the back at D, four canvas threads above A. Pull the thread through.

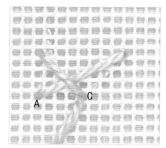

5 Re-emerge at C, taking care not to split the thread. Pull the thread through.

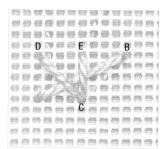

6 Take the needle to the back at E, four canvas threads above C. Pull the thread through.

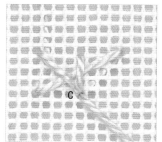

7 To begin the second stitch, bring the thread to the front at C, taking care not to split the thread. Pull the thread through.

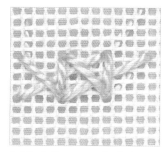

8 Work the second stitch following steps 2–6.

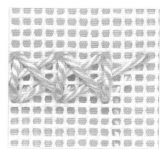

9 Working from left to right, continue working stitches across the row.

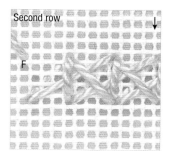

10 Turn the canvas upside down. Bring the thread to the front at F, four canvas threads above the lower left corner of the previous stitch.

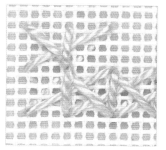

11 Work the stitch following steps 2–4. Take care not to split the thread in the shared holes.

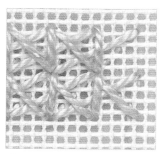

12 Working from left to right, work stitches across the row in the same manner. Take care not to split the thread in the shared holes.

CROSS STITCH – MONTENEGRIN / CONTINUED

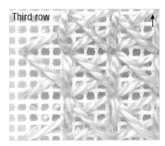

13 Continue working rows of stitches in the same manner, turning the canvas after each one.

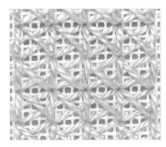

14 Turn the canvas upside down. Stitch the third row in exactly the same manner as the first row.

Heaven Scent

CROSS STITCH – OBLONG

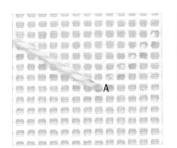

1 Secure the thread on the upper right hand side. Bring it to the front at A, the base of the stitch.

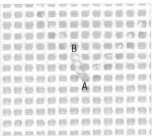

2 Take the needle to the back at B, two canvas threads above and one canvas thread to the left. Pull the thread through.

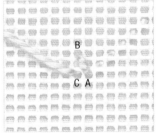

3 Re-emerge at C, one canvas thread to the left of A. Pull the thread through.

4 Take the needle to the back at D, two canvas threads above and one canvas thread to the left. Pull the thread through.

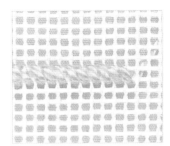

5 Working from right to left, continue working diagonal stitches across the row.

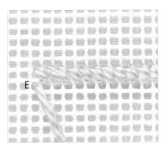

6 Re-emerge at E, two canvas threads directly below the tip of the last stitch. Pull the thread through.

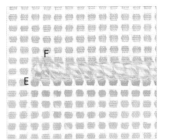

7 Take the needle to the back at F, two canvas threads above and one canvas thread to the right of E. Pull thread through.

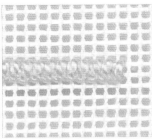

8 Working from left to right, continue working diagonal stitches across the row.

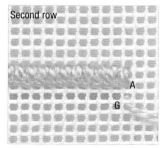

9 Bring the needle to the front at G, two canvas threads below A. Pull the thread through.

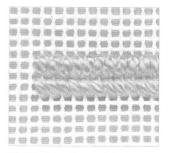

10 Working from right to left, work diagonal stitches across the row in the same manner as before.

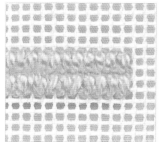

11 Working from left to right, work diagonal stitches back across the row in the same manner as before.

12 Continue working rows of stitches, back and forth, across the canvas.

CROSS STITCH – TWO-SIDED

Two-sided cross stitch is also known as Italian cross stitch and arrowhead cross stitch.

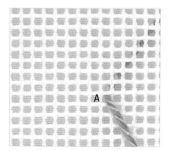

1 Secure the thread on the upper right hand side. Bring it to the front at A.

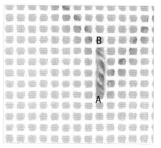

2 Take the needle to the back at B, four canvas threads above. Pull the thread through.

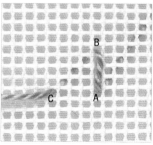

3 Re-emerge at C, four canvas threads to the left of A. Pull the thread through.

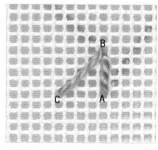

4 Take the needle to the back at B again. Pull the thread through.

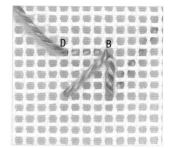

5 Re-emerge at D, four canvas threads to the left of B. Pull the thread through.

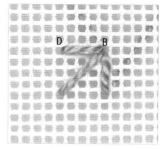

6 Take the needle to the back at B again. Pull the thread through.

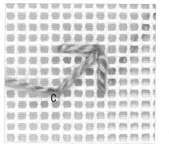

7 To begin the second repeat, bring the needle to the front at C. Pull the thread through.

8 Work the stitch following steps 2–6.

↑ Indicates top of canvas

9 Working from right to left, continue working stitches across the row.

10 Turn the canvas upside down. Bring the thread to the front in the lower right hand corner of the last repeat.

11 Take the needle to the back in the upper left hand corner of the repeat.

12 Pull the thread through to form a diagonal stitch. Re-emerge at the bottom right hand corner of the next repeat.

13 Working from right to left, work diagonal stitches across the row in the same manner.

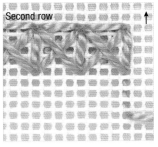

14 Turn the canvas upside down. Bring the thread to the front four canvas threads below the right hand end of the last stitch.

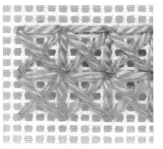

15 Working from right to left, work the row in the same manner as before, turning the canvas to work the second section.

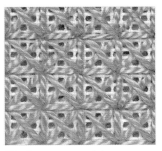

16 Continue working rows of stitches in the same manner, turning the canvas after each section.

CROSS STITCH – UPRIGHT

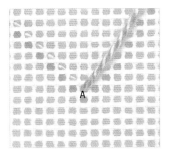

1 Secure the thread on the upper left hand side. Bring it to the front at A, the base of the stitch.

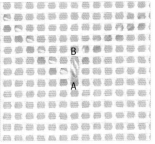

2 Crossing two canvas threads, take the needle to the back at B, directly above. Pull the thread through.

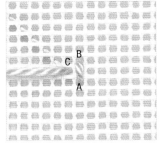

3 Re-emerge at C, one canvas thread to the left and halfway between A and B. Pull the thread through.

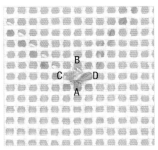

4 Take the thread to the back at D, two canvas threads to the right of C. Pull the thread through.

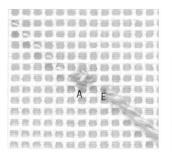

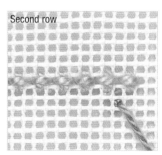
Second row

5 To begin the second stitch, bring the needle to the front at E, two canvas threads to the right of A. Pull the thread through.

6 Work the second stitch following steps 2–5. Take care not to split the thread in the shared hole on the left hand side.

7 Continue working stitches across the row in the same manner.

8 Bring the needle to the front one canvas thread below and to the left of the base of the last stitch. Pull the thread through.

Third row

9 Work the stitch following steps 2–5. Take care not to split the thread in the shared holes.

10 Working from right to left, continue working stitches across the row.

11 Working from left to right, work a third row of stitches.

12 Continue working rows of stitches, back and forth, across the canvas.

CUSHION STITCH

See Scottish stitch on pages 105–106.

Evergreen

DARNING STITCH

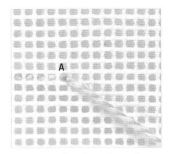

1 Secure the thread on the upper left hand side. Bring it to the front at A.

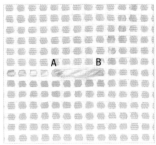

2 Take the needle to the back at B, four canvas threads to the right. Pull the thread through.

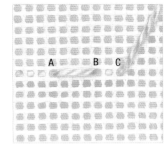

3 Re-emerge at C, two canvas threads to the right. Pull the thread through.

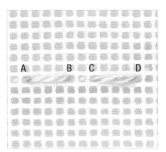

4 Take the needle to the back at D, four canvas threads to the right. Pull the thread through.

5 Continue in this manner to the end of the row.

6 Bring the needle to the front through the same hole as the beginning of the last stitch. Pull the thread through.

7 Take the needle to the back two canvas threads to the left (the same hole as the end of the second to last stitch). Pull the thread through.

8 Working from right to left, continue working stitches in each space across the row.

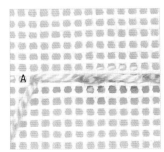

9 Bring the needle to the front at A, just under the first stitch. Take care not to split the thread in the shared hole.

10 Repeat steps 2–8 back and forth across the row.

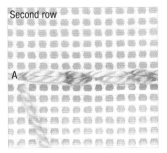

11 Bring the thread to the front one canvas thread below A.

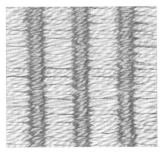

12 Continue working rows of stitches, back and forth across the canvas, in the same manner.

41

DIAGONAL STITCH

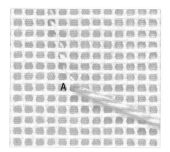

1 Secure the thread on the upper left hand side. Bring it to the front at A.

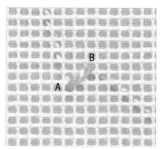

2 Crossing two canvas intersections, take the needle to the back at B, above and to the right. Pull the thread through.

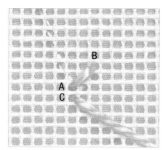

3 Re-emerge at C, one canvas thread below A. Pull the thread through.

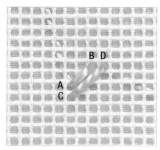

4 Take the needle to the back at D, one canvas thread to the right of B. Pull the thread through.

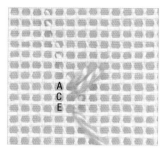

5 Re-emerge at E, one canvas thread below C. Pull the thread through.

6 Take the needle to the back at F, one canvas thread to the right of D. Pull the thread through.

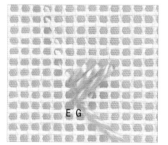

7 Re-emerge at G, one canvas thread to the right of E. Pull the thread through.

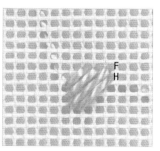

8 Take the needle to the back at H, one canvas thread below F. Pull the thread through.

9 To begin the second stitch, bring the thread to the front at I, one canvas thread to the right of G. Pull the thread through.

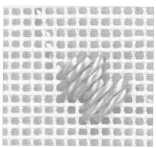

10 Work the second stitch following steps 2–8.

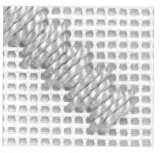

11 Working diagonally from left to right, continue working stitches across the row.

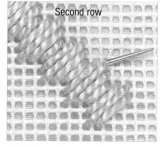

12 Bring the needle to the front through the same hole as the tip of the longest straight stitch in the second to last diagonal stitch worked.

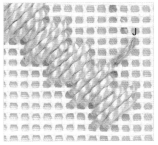

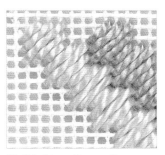

13 Pull the thread through. Crossing two canvas intersections, take the needle to the back at J, above and to the right. Pull the thread through.

14 Complete the stitch in a similar manner to before.

15 Working diagonally from right to left, work stitches across the row in the same manner. Take care not to split the thread in the shared holes.

16 Continue working rows of stitches, diagonally back and forth, across the canvas.

Bargello embroidery

This form of needlepoint is also known as Florentine work, flame work and Hungarian point.

The name originates from a series of chairs found in the Bargello palace in Florence, Italy, which had a flame stitch pattern. This palace was built in 1255 to host the Florence City Council. Later, it was employed as a prison, with executions taking place in the Bargello's yard until 1786.

Traditionally there existed two styles of embroidery with very similar characteristics that originated in different countries. Bargello was invented in Italy and utilized vertical stitches of exactly the same height, which were offset from the previous stitch by two or more threads. Hungarian point originated in Hungary and utilized short stitches alternated with longer stitches. Both styles are very colourful and use many shades of one colour. The patterns are naturally geometric and many are based on three traditional patterns – the diamond motif known as Puzta or feathered carnation; the 'V' or lightning motif which is often called Blitz Troellakan; and the wave motif which is similar to the 'V' motif but is curved rather than jagged.

In most traditional pieces, all stitches are vertical. Modern bargello also often incorporates horizontal stitches.

This remarkably durable form of embroidery is well suited for use on cushions, upholstery, purses, bags and even carpets.

DIAMOND EYELET STITCH

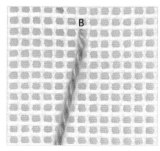

1 Secure the thread on the upper left hand side. Bring it to the front at B, the top of the stitch.

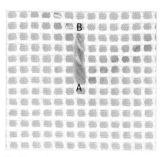

2 Crossing four canvas threads, take the needle to the back at A, below. Pull the thread through.

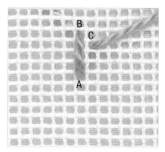

3 Re-emerge at C, one canvas intersection below and to the right of B. Pull the thread through.

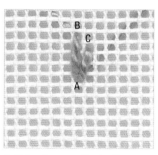

4 Take the needle to the back at A, taking care not to split the thread. Pull the thread through.

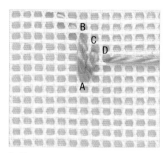

5 Re-emerge at D, one canvas intersection below and to the right of C. Pull the thread through.

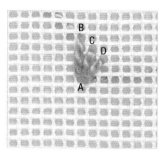

6 Take the needle to the back at A, taking care not to split the thread. Pull the thread through.

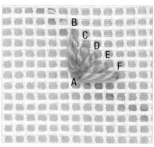

7 Work two more stitches in the same manner, always emerging one canvas intersection below and to the right of the previous stitch (E and F).

8 Re-emerge at G, one canvas intersection below and to the left of F. Pull the thread through.

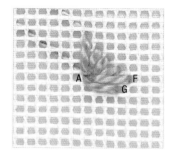

9 Take the needle to the back at A, taking care not to split the thread. Pull the thread through.

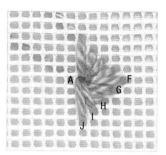

10 Work three more stitches in the same manner, always emerging one canvas intersection below and to the left of the previous stitch (H, I and J).

11 Re-emerge at K, one canvas intersection above and to the left of J. Pull the thread through.

12 Take the needle to the back at A, taking care not to split the thread. Pull the thread through.

13 Work three more stitches in the same manner, always emerging one canvas intersection above and to the left of the previous stitch (L, M and N).

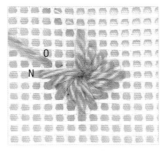

14 Re-emerge at O, one canvas intersection above and to the right of N. Pull the thread through.

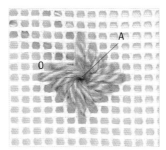

15 Take the needle to the back at A, taking care not to split the thread. Pull the thread through.

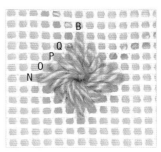

16 Work two more stitches in the same manner, always emerging one canvas intersection above and to the right of the previous stitch (P and Q).

17 To begin the second stitch, bring the thread to the front at R, eight canvas threads to the right of B.

18 Work the second stitch following steps 2–16.

19 Working from left to right, continue working stitches across the row.

Second row

20 Bring the needle to the front halfway between the last two diamond eyelet stitches as shown.

21 Work the stitch following steps 2–16. Take care not to split the thread in the shared holes.

22 Working from right to left, work stitches across the row in the same manner. Take care not to split the thread in the shared holes.

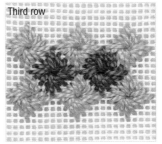

Third row

23 Stitch the third row in exactly the same manner as the first row.

24 Continue working rows of stitches, back and forth, across the canvas.

EGGS-IN-A-BASKET STITCH

Note the canvas is positioned on the diagonal for this stitch.

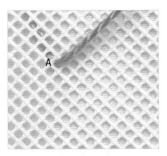

1 Secure the thread. Bring it to the front at A, near the middle of the stitch on the left hand side.

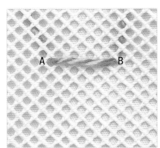

2 Crossing four canvas intersections, take the needle to the back at B. Pull the thread through.

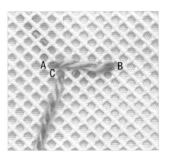

3 Re-emerge at C, one canvas thread below and to the right of A. Pull the thread through.

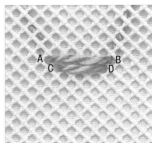

4 Crossing three canvas intersections, take the needle to the back at D, just below and to the left of B. Pull the thread through.

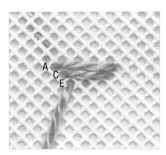

5 Re-emerge at E, one canvas thread below and to the right of C. Pull the thread through.

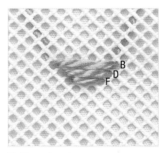

6 Crossing two canvas intersections, take the needle to the back at F, just below and to the left of D. Pull the thread through.

7 Re-emerge at G, one canvas thread below and to the right of E. Pull the thread through.

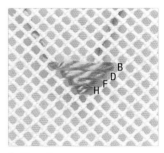

8 Crossing one canvas intersection, take the needle to the back at H, just below and to the left of F. Pull the thread through.

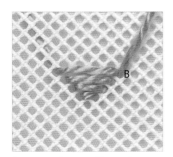

9 Bring the needle to the front at B to begin the second basket. Pull the thread through.

10 Work the second basket, following steps 2–8.

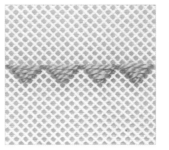

11 Continue working baskets across the row in the same manner.

12 To begin the eggs, bring the needle to the front at J, just above the basket. Pull the thread through.

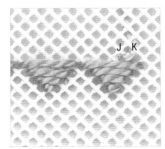

13 Take the needle to the back at K, one canvas thread to the right. Pull the thread through.

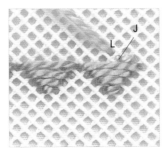

14 Re-emerge at L, one canvas thread above and to the left of J. Pull the thread through.

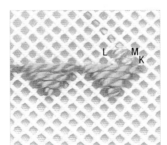

15 Take the needle to the back at M, one canvas thread above and to the left of K. Pull the thread through.

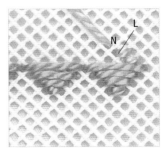

16 Re-emerge at N, one canvas thread above and to the left of L. Pull the thread through.

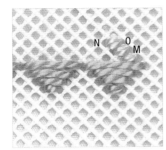

17 Take the needle to the back at O, one canvas thread above and to the left of M. Pull the thread through.

18 Re-emerge at P, one canvas thread to the left of J. Pull the thread through.

19 Crossing one canvas thread to the right, take the needle to the back at J. Pull the thread through.

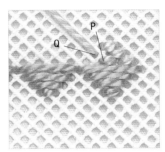

20 Re-emerge at Q, one canvas thread above and to the left of P. Pull the thread through.

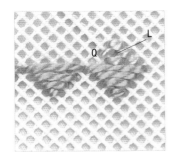

21 Crossing one canvas thread to the right, take the needle to the back at L. Pull the thread through.

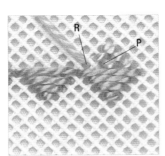

22 Re-emerge at R, one canvas thread to the left of P. Pull the thread through.

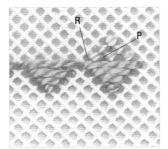

23 Crossing one canvas thread to the right, take the needle to the back at P. Pull the thread through.

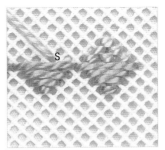

24 Bring the needle to the front at S to begin the eggs in the second basket. Pull the thread through.

25 Work the eggs, following steps 13–23.

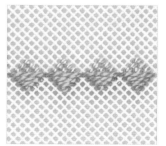

26 Continue working eggs across the row in the same manner.

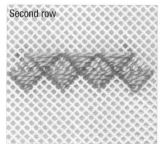

Second row

27 Beginning on the left hand side, work a second row of baskets, placing them between the eggs of the first row.

28 Beginning on the right hand side, work the eggs of the second row of baskets.

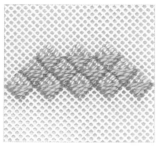

29 Continue working rows of baskets and eggs back and forth across the canvas.

30 To create a straight edge, fill the triangles between the piles of eggs with 'empty' baskets and vice versa.

English needlepoint chair seat c1730

EYELET STITCH

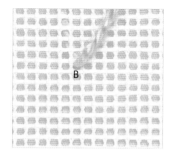

1 Secure the thread. Bring it to the front at B, on the upper left hand side.

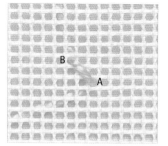

2 Take the needle to the back at A, two canvas intersections below and to the right of B. Pull the thread through.

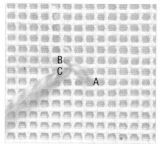

3 Re-emerge at C, one canvas thread below B. Pull the thread through.

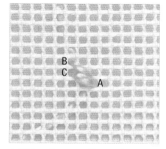

4 Take the needle to the back at A again. Pull the thread through.

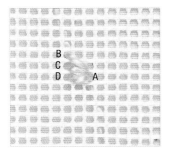

5 Re-emerge at D, one canvas thread below C. Pull the thread through. Take the needle to the back at A again. Pull the thread through.

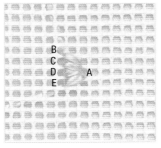

6 Re-emerge at E, one canvas thread below D. Pull the thread through. Take the needle to the back at A again. Pull the thread through.

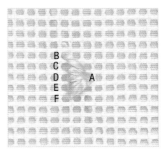

7 Re-emerge at F, one canvas thread below E. Pull the thread through. Take the needle to the back at A again. Pull the thread through.

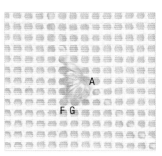

8 Re-emerge at G, one canvas thread to the right of F. Pull the thread through. Take the needle to the back at A again. Pull the thread through.

9 Work three more stitches, moving one canvas thread to the right for each stitch, in the same manner (H, I and J).

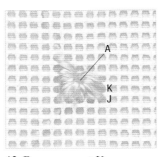

10 Re-emerge at K, one canvas thread above J. Pull the thread through. Take the needle to the back at A again. Pull the thread through.

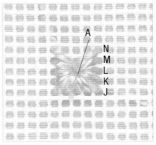

11 Work three more stitches in the same manner, moving one canvas thread above for each stitch (L, M and N).

12 Re-emerge at O, one canvas thread to the left of N. Pull the thread through. Take the needle to the back at A again. Pull the thread through.

13 Work two more stitches in the same manner, moving one canvas thread to the left for each stitch (P and Q).

14 To begin the second stitch, bring the needle to the front at N. Take care not to split the thread in the shared hole.

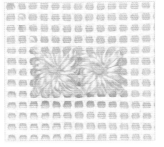

15 Pull the thread through. Work the second stitch, following steps 2–13.

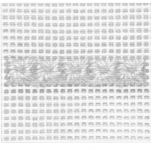

16 Continue working stitches from left to right across the row in the same manner.

49

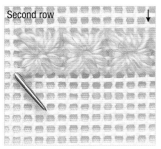

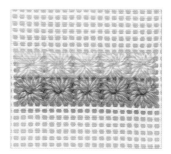

17 Turn the canvas upside down. Bring the needle to the front through the same hole as the lower left hand corner of the previous stitch.

18 Pull the thread through. Work the stitch, following steps 2–13.

19 Continue working stitches, from left to right, across the row in the same manner.

20 Continue working rows of stitches in the same manner, turning the canvas after each one.

FAN STITCH

See ray stitch on pages 91–92.

FERN STITCH

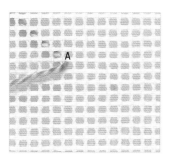

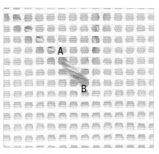

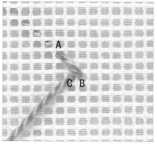

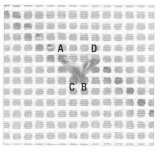

1 Secure the thread. Bring it to the front at A, on the upper left hand side.

2 Crossing two canvas intersections, take the needle to the back at B, below and to the right. Pull the thread through.

3 Re-emerge at C, one canvas thread to the left of B. Pull the thread through.

4 Take the needle to the back at D, three canvas threads to the right of A. Pull the thread through.

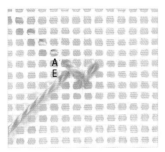

5 To begin the second stitch, bring the needle to the front at E, one canvas thread below A. Pull the thread through.

6 Work the second stitch, following steps 2–4.

7 Continue working stitches down the row in the same manner.

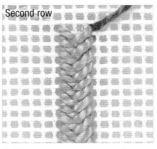

8 Return to the top and bring the needle to the front at D. Pull the thread through.

9 Work stitches downwards in the same manner as the first row. Take care not to split the thread in the shared holes.

10 Continue working rows of stitches down the canvas.

English needlework chairs, c1720

FISHBONE STITCH

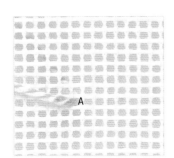

1 Secure the thread. Bring it to the front at A, on the upper left hand side.

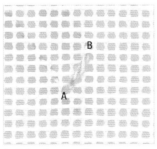

2 Take the needle to the back at B, three canvas threads above and two canvas threads to the right of A. Pull the thread through.

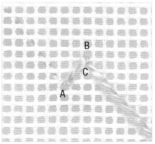

3 Re-emerge at C, one canvas thread below B. Pull the thread through.

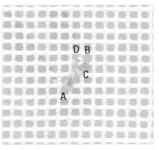

4 Take the needle to the back at D, one canvas thread to the left of B. Pull the thread through.

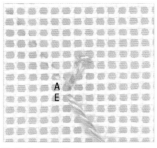

5 To begin the second stitch, bring the needle to the front at E, one canvas thread below A.

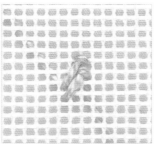

6 Work the second stitch, following steps 2–4.

7 Continue working stitches down the row in the same manner.

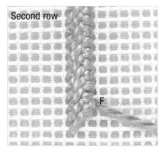

8 Bring the needle to the front through the same hole as the tip of the previous stitch (F). Pull the thread through.

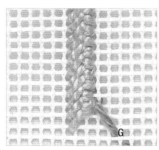

9 Take the needle to the back at G, four canvas threads to the right of the base of the previous stitch. Pull the thread through.

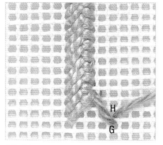

10 Re-emerge at H, one canvas thread above G. Pull the thread through.

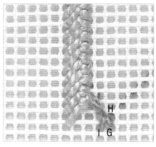

11 Take the needle to the back at I, one canvas thread to the left of G. Pull the thread through.

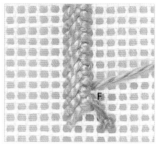

12 To begin the second stitch, bring the needle to the front one canvas thread above F.

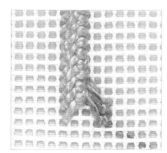

13 Work the second stitch, following steps 9–11.

14 Continue working stitches up the row in the same manner.

15 Work the third row in exactly the same manner as the first row.

16 Continue working rows of stitches up and down the canvas.

FLORENTINE STITCH

Florentine stitch is also known as flame stitch. It has many variations, which are created by varying the length and number of straight stitches in each repeat.

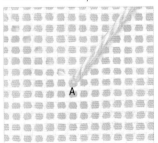

1 Secure the thread. Bring it to the front at A, on the right hand side.

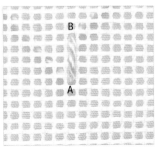

2 Take the needle to the back at B, four canvas threads above A. Pull the thread through.

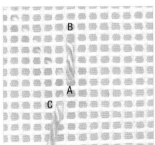

3 Re-emerge at C, two canvas threads below and one canvas thread to the left of A. Pull the thread through.

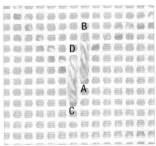

4 Take the needle to the back at D, four canvas threads above C. Pull the thread through.

5 Repeat steps 3–4 twice to form two more stepped stitches.

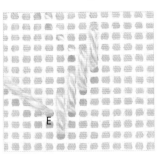

6 Bring the needle to the front at E, two canvas threads above and one to the left of the base of the previous stitch. Pull the thread through.

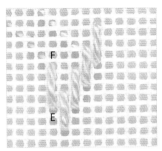

7 Take the needle to the back at F, four canvas threads above E. Pull the thread through.

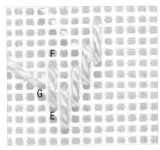

8 Re-emerge at G, two canvas threads above and one canvas thread to the left of E. Pull the thread through.

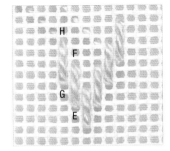

9 Take the needle to the back at H, four canvas threads above G. Pull the thread through.

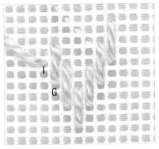

10 To repeat the sequence, bring the needle to the front at I, two canvas threads above and one to the left of G. Pull the thread through.

11 Repeat steps 2–9.

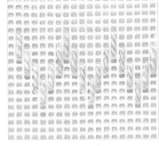

12 Continue working stitches from right to left across the row in the same manner.

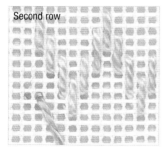

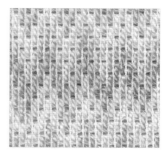

13 Bring the needle to the front four canvas threads below the base of the last stitch. Pull the thread through.

14 Take the thread to the back at the base of the last stitch of the previous row.

15 Working from left to right, stitch vertical straight stitches across the row, maintaining the pattern of the first row. Take care not to split the thread in the shared holes.

16 Continue working rows of stitches, back and forth, across the canvas.

Examples of florentine work

FRENCH STITCH

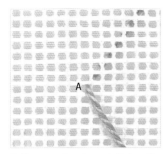

1 Secure the thread. Bring it to the front at A, on the right hand side.

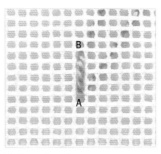

2 Crossing four canvas threads, take the needle to the back at B, directly above. Pull the thread through.

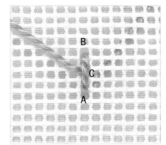

3 Keeping the needle to the left of the existing thread, re-emerge at C, through the hole halfway between A and B. Pull the thread through.

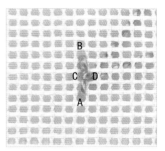

4 Take the needle to the back at D, one canvas thread to the right of C. Pull the thread through to form a short horizontal stitch.

5 Re-emerge at A, keeping the thread to the left of the previous thread in the same hole. Pull the thread through.

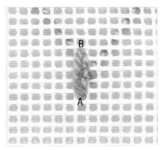

6 Take the needle to the back at B, keeping the thread to the left of the previous thread in the same hole. Pull the thread through.

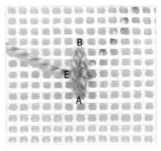

7 Re-emerge at E, one canvas thread to the left and halfway between A and B. Pull the thread through.

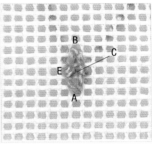

8 Take the needle to the back at C, one canvas thread to the right of E. Pull the thread through to form a short horizontal stitch.

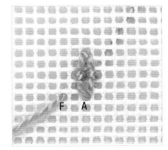

9 To begin the second stitch, bring the needle to the front at F, two canvas threads to the left of A. Pull the thread through.

10 Work the second stitch, following steps 2–8.

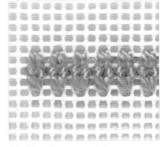

11 Continue working stitches across the row in the same manner.

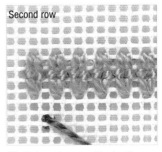

12 Bring the needle to the front two canvas threads below and one canvas thread to the right of the base of the last stitch. Pull the thread through.

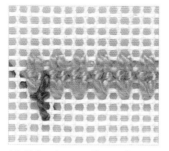

13 Work a long vertical straight stitch as before. Bring the needle to the front halfway along the vertical stitch and just on the right hand side of it. Pull the thread through.

14 Take the needle to the back, one canvas thread to the left. Pull the thread through.

15 Work a second long vertical straight stitch as before.

16 Re-emerge one canvas thread to the right of the previous short horizontal stitch. Pull the thread through.

17 Take the needle to the back over one canvas thread to the left, anchoring the vertical stitch.

18 Work stitches, from left to right, across the row in the same manner as before.

The Bradford Carpet

The Bradford Carpet, housed in the Victoria and Albert Museum, is a fine example of Elizabethan canvaswork. It was made in the late 17th century and was originally the property of the Earl of Bradford at Castle Bromwich.

Measuring 4m × 1.75m wide (4yd 12" × 1yd 33"), the carpet was made neither for wall nor floor, but as a table covering. Twenty-three silk threads were worked onto a linen canvas to show the rural life of the times in a simple but realistic way.

It was stitched in tent stitch with 400 stitches to the square inch (20 count canvas), and it is believed to have been made by professionals, not the household.

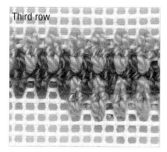

19 Work a third row, from right to left, across the canvas.

20 Continue working rows of stitches, back and forth, across the canvas.

Detail of the carpet

GOBELIN STITCH – ENCROACHING

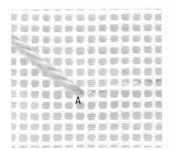

1 Secure the thread. Bring it to the front at A, on the upper right hand side.

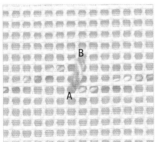

2 Take the needle to the back at B, three canvas threads above and one canvas thread to the right of A. Pull the thread through.

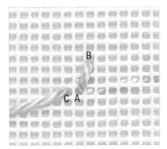

3 Re-emerge at C, one canvas thread to the left of A. Pull the thread through.

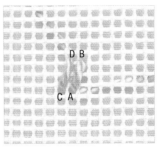

4 Take the needle to the back at D, one canvas thread to the left of B. Pull the thread through.

5 Continue working stitches from right to left across the row in the same manner.

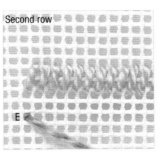

6 Bring the needle to the front two canvas threads below the lower end of the last stitch (E). Pull the thread through.

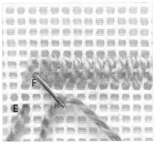

7 Take the needle to the back at F, three canvas threads above and one to the right of E. This is between the last and second to last stitches of the previous row.

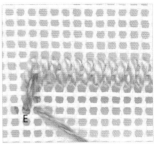

8 Pull the thread through. Re-emerge one canvas thread to the right of E and pull the thread through.

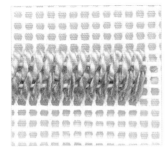

9 Continue working stitches, from left to right, across the row in the same manner.

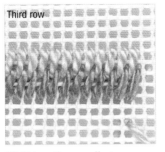

10 Bring the needle to the front two canvas threads below the lower end of the last stitch. Pull the thread through.

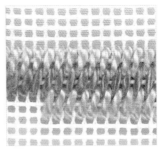

11 Work stitches, from right to left, across the row in the same manner as before.

12 Continue working rows of stitches, back and forth, across the canvas.

GOBELIN STITCH – PLAITED

1 Secure the thread. Bring it to the front at A, on the upper right hand side.

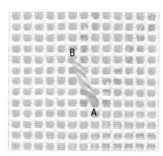

2 Take the needle to the back at B, four canvas threads above and two canvas threads to the left of A. Pull the thread through.

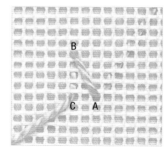

3 Re-emerge at C, two canvas threads to the left of A. Pull the thread through

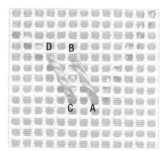

4 Take the needle to the back at D, two canvas threads to the left of B. Pull the thread through.

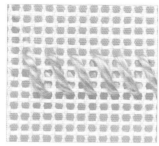

5 Continue working stitches from right to left across the row in the same manner.

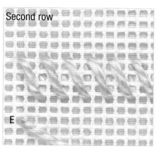

6 Bring the needle to the front six canvas threads below the upper end of the last stitch (E). Pull the thread through.

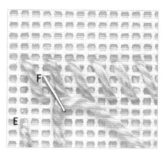

7 Take the needle to the back at F, four canvas threads above and two canvas threads to the right of E.

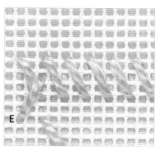

8 Pull the thread through. Re-emerge two canvas threads to the right of E and pull the thread through.

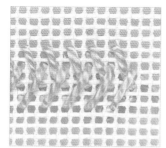

9 Continue working stitches, from left to right, across the row in the same manner.

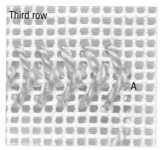

10 Bring the needle to the front four canvas threads below A. Pull the thread through.

11 Work stitches, from right to left, across the row in the same manner as before. The tops of the stitches share the same holes as the bottoms of the stitches of the first row.

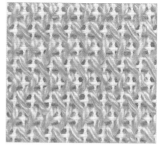

12 Continue working rows of stitches, back and forth, across the canvas.

GOBELIN STITCH – SLANTED

1 Secure the thread. Bring it to the front at A, on the upper right hand side.

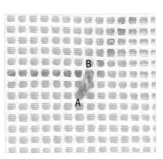

2 Take the needle to the back at B, two canvas threads above and one canvas thread to the right of A. Pull the thread through.

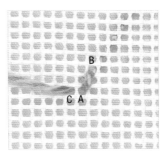

3 Re-emerge at C, one canvas thread to the left of A. Pull the thread through.

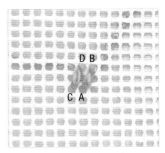

4 Take the needle to the back at D, one canvas thread to the left of B. Pull the thread through.

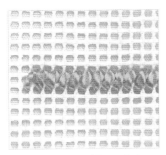

5 Continue working stitches from right to left across the row in the same manner.

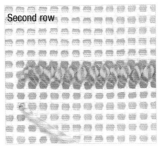

6 Bring the needle to the front two canvas threads below the lower end of the last stitch. Pull the thread through.

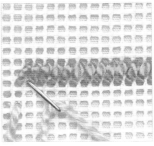

7 Take the needle to the back through the same hole as the lower end of the second to last stitch in the previous row.

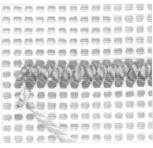

8 Pull the thread through. Re-emerge one canvas thread across from the lower end of the first stitch in this row and pull the thread through.

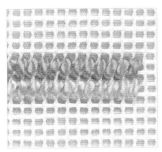

9 Continue working stitches, from left to right, across the row in the same manner.

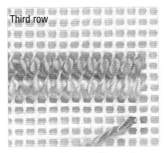

10 Bring the needle to the front two canvas threads below the lower end of the last stitch. Pull the thread through.

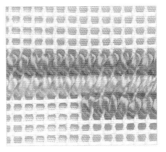

11 Work stitches, from right to left, across the row in the same manner as before.

12 Continue working rows of stitches, back and forth, across the canvas.

GOBELIN STITCH – STRAIGHT

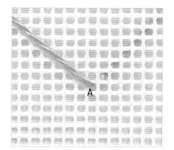

1 Secure the thread. Bring it to the front at A, on the right hand side.

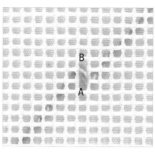

2 Crossing two canvas threads, take the needle to the back at B, directly above. Pull the thread through.

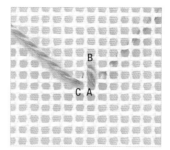

3 Re-emerge at C, one canvas thread to the left of A. Pull the thread through.

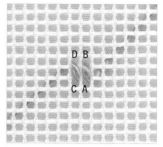

4 Take the needle to the back at D, one canvas thread to the left of B. Pull the thread through.

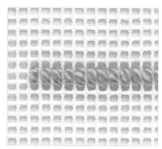

5 Continue working stitches from right to left across the row in the same manner.

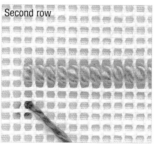

6 Bring the needle to the front two canvas threads below the lower end of the last stitch. Pull the thread through.

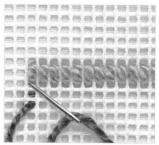

7 Take the needle to the back through the same hole as the lower end of the last stitch in the previous row.

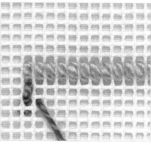

8 Pull the thread through. Re-emerge one canvas thread across from the lower end of the first stitch in this row and pull the thread through.

9 Continue working stitches, from left to right, across the row in the same manner.

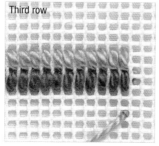

10 Bring the needle to the front two canvas threads below the lower end of the last stitch. Pull the thread through.

11 Work stitches, from right to left, across the row in the same manner as before.

12 Continue working rows of stitches, back and forth, across the canvas.

GREEK STITCH

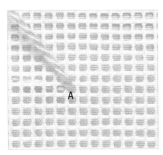

1 Secure the thread on the upper left hand side. Bring it to the front at A, the base of the stitch.

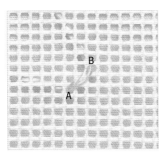

2 Crossing two canvas intersections, take the needle to the back at B, above and to the right of A. Pull the thread through.

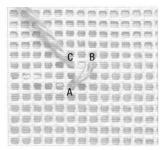

3 Re-emerge at C, two canvas threads to the left of B. Pull the thread through.

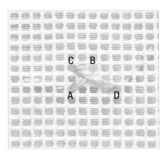

4 Take the needle to the back at D, four canvas threads to the right of A. Pull the thread through.

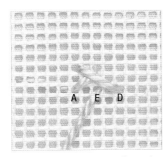

5 To begin the second stitch, bring the needle to the front at E, two canvas threads to the left of D. Pull the thread through.

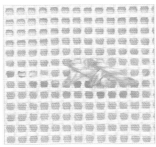

6 Work the second stitch following steps 2–4.

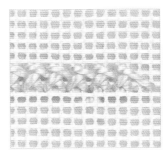

7 Working from left to right, continue working stitches across the row.

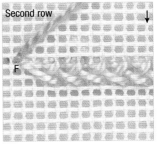

8 Turn the canvas upside down. Bring the needle to the front at F, through the same hole as the tip of the long arm of the previous stitch.

9 Work the stitch following steps 2–4. Take care not to split the thread in the shared holes.

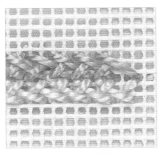

10 Working from left to right, work stitches across the row in the same manner. Take care not to split the thread in the shared holes.

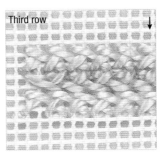

11 Turn the canvas upside down. Stitch the third row in exactly the same manner as the first row.

12 Continue working rows of stitches in the same manner, turning the canvas after each one.

HERRINGBONE STITCH

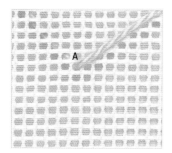

1 Secure the thread. Bring it to the front at A, on the upper left hand side.

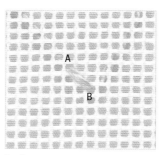

2 Crossing two canvas intersections, take the needle to the back at B, below and to the right of A. Pull the thread through.

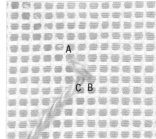

3 Re-emerge at C, one canvas thread to the left of B. Pull the thread through.

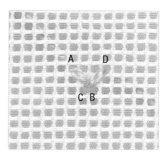

4 Crossing two canvas intersections, take the needle to the back at D, above and to the right of C. Pull the thread through.

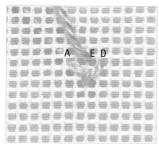

5 To begin the second stitch, bring the needle to the front at E, one canvas thread to the left of D. Pull the thread through.

6 Work the second stitch following steps 2–4.

7 Continue working stitches from left to right across the row in the same manner.

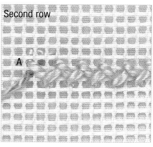

8 Bring the needle to the front one canvas thread below A. Pull the thread through.

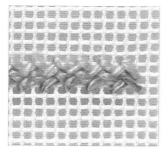

9 Work stitches, from left to right, across the row in the same manner as before.

10 Continue working rows of stitches, from left to right, across the canvas.

18th century French needlework picture

HERRINGBONE STITCH - DOUBLE

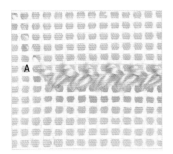

1 Secure the thread. Bring it to the front at A, on the left hand side. Stitch the first row, following steps 2–7 for Herringbone stitch on page 62.

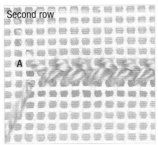

2 Return to the left hand side. Bring the needle to the front two canvas threads below A. Pull the thread through.

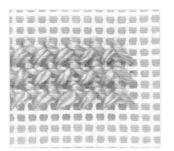

3 Work across the row in the same manner as before. Continue working rows of stitches, from left to right, across the canvas.

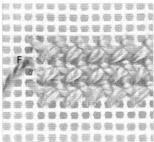

4 Using a new thread, bring it to the front at F. Take care not to split the thread in the shared hole. Pull the thread through.

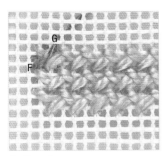

5 Crossing two canvas intersections, take the needle to the back at G, above and to the right of F. Pull the thread through.

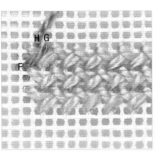

6 Re-emerge at H, one canvas thread to the left of G. Pull the thread through.

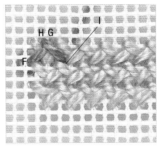

7 Crossing two canvas intersections, take the needle to the back at I, below and to the right of H. Pull the thread through.

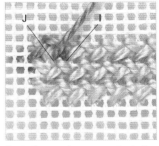

8 To begin the second stitch, bring the needle to the front at J, one canvas thread to the left of I. Pull the thread through.

9 Repeat steps 5–8 across the row. Take care not to split the thread in the shared holes.

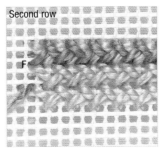

10 Return to the left hand side. Bring the needle to the front two canvas threads below F. Pull the thread through.

11 Work stitches, from left to right, across the row in the same manner as before.

12 Continue working rows of stitches, from left to right, across the canvas.

HUNGARIAN STITCH

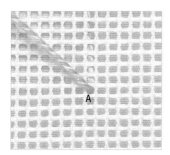

1 Secure the thread. Bring it to the front at A, on the upper right hand side.

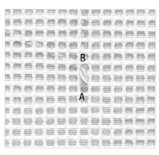

2 Crossing two canvas threads, take the needle to the back at B, directly above. Pull the thread through.

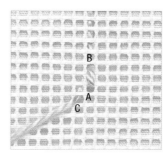

3 Re-emerge at C, one canvas intersection below and to the left of A. Pull the thread through.

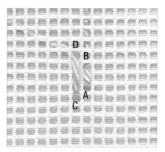

4 Take the needle to the back at D, one canvas intersection above and to the left of B. Pull the thread through.

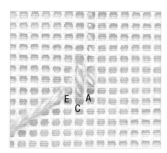

5 Re-emerge at E, one canvas intersection above and to the left of C. Pull the thread through.

6 Take the needle to the back at F, one canvas intersection below and to the left of D. Pull the thread through.

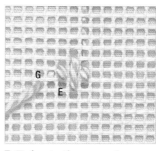

7 To begin the second stitch, bring the needle to the front at G, two canvas threads to the left of E. Pull the thread through.

8 Work the second stitch following steps 2–6.

9 Continue working stitches from right to left across the row in the same manner.

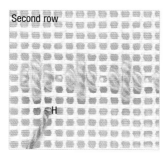

10 Bring the needle to the front two canvas threads below the lower end of the third to last stitch (H). Pull the thread through.

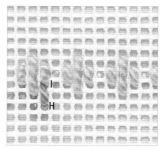

11 Take the needle to the back through the same hole as the lower end of the third to last stitch in the previous row (I).

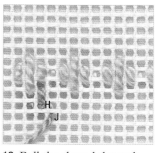

12 Pull the thread through. Re-emerge at J, one canvas intersection below and to the right of H. Pull the thread through.

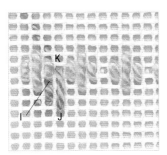

13 Take the needle to the back at K, one canvas intersection above and to the right of I. Pull the thread through.

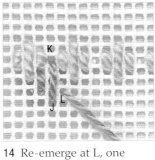

14 Re-emerge at L, one canvas intersection above and to the right of J. Pull the thread through.

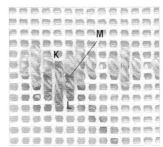

15 Take the needle to the back at M, one canvas intersection below and to the right of K. Pull the thread through.

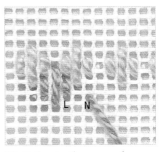

16 To begin the second stitch, bring the needle to the front at N, two canvas threads to the right of L. Pull the thread through.

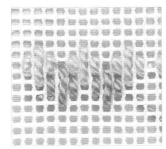

17 Work the second stitch following steps 11–15.

18 Continue working stitches, from left to right, across the row in the same manner.

19 Work the third row in the same manner as the first row.

20 Continue working rows of stitches, back and forth, across the canvas.

HUNGARIAN DIAMOND STITCH

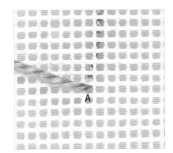

1 Secure the thread. Bring it to the front at A, on the upper right hand side.

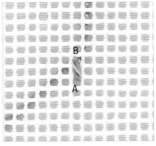

2 Crossing two canvas threads, take the needle to the back at B, directly above. Pull the thread through.

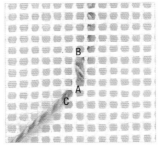

3 Re-emerge at C, one canvas intersection below and to the left of A. Pull the thread through.

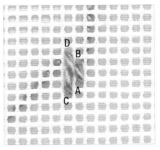

4 Take the needle to the back at D, one canvas intersection above and to the left of B. Pull the thread through.

5 Re-emerge at E, one canvas intersection below and to the left of C. Pull the thread through.

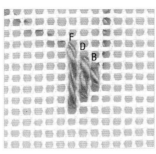

6 Take the needle to the back at F, one canvas intersection above and to the left of D. Pull the thread through.

7 Re-emerge at G, one canvas intersection above and to the left of E. Pull the thread through.

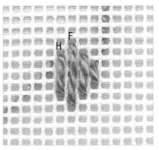

8 Take the needle to the back at H, one canvas intersection below and to the left of F. Pull the thread through.

9 Re-emerge at I, one canvas intersection above and to the left of G. Pull the thread through.

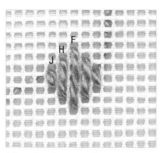

10 Take the needle to the back at J, one canvas intersection below and to the left of H. Pull the thread through.

11 To begin the second stitch, bring the needle to the front at K, two canvas threads to the left of I. Pull the thread through.

12 Work the second stitch following steps 2–10.

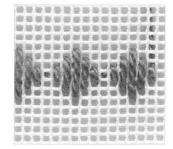

13 Continue working stitches, from right to left, across the row in the same manner.

14 Bring the needle to the front two canvas threads below the lower end of the fourth to last stitch (L). Pull the thread through.

15 Take the needle to the back through the same hole as the lower end of the fourth to last stitch in the previous row (M).

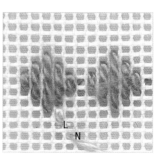

16 Pull the thread through. Re-emerge at N, one canvas intersection below and to the right of L. Pull the thread through.

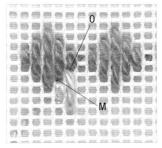

17 Take the needle to the back at O, one canvas intersection above and to the right of M. Pull the thread through.

18 Re-emerge at P, one canvas intersection below and to the right of N. Pull the thread through.

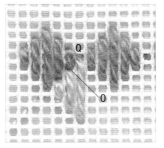

19 Take the needle to the back at Q, one canvas intersection above and to the right of O. Pull the thread through.

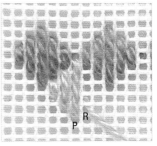

20 Re-emerge at R, one canvas intersection above and to the right of P. Pull the thread through.

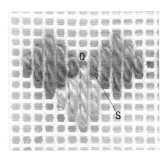

21 Take the needle to the back at S, one canvas intersection below and to the right of Q. Pull the thread through.

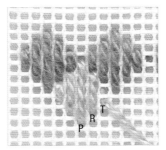

22 Re-emerge at T, one canvas intersection above and to the right of R. Pull the thread through.

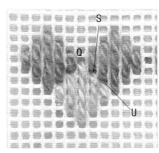

23 Take the needle to the back at U, one canvas intersection below and to the right of S. Pull the thread through.

24 To begin the second stitch, bring the needle to the front at V, two canvas threads to the right of T. Pull the thread through.

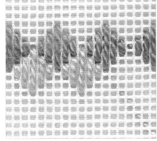

25 Work the second stitch following steps 15–23.

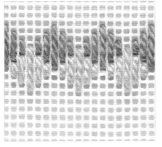

26 Continue working stitches, from left to right, across the row in the same manner.

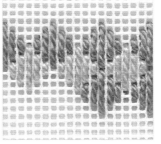

27 Work the third row in the same manner as the first row.

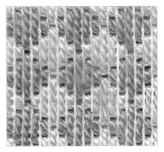

28 Continue working rows of stitches, back and forth, across the canvas.

JACQUARD STITCH

The rows of longer stitches are worked in a similar manner to Byzantine stitch. Rows of continental stitch are worked in between.

1 Secure the thread on the upper left hand side. Bring it to the front at A.

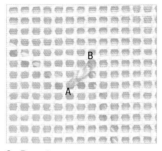

2 Crossing two canvas intersections, take the needle to the back at B, diagonally above and to the right. Pull the thread through.

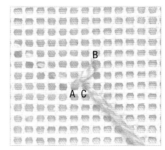

3 Re-emerge at C, one canvas thread to the right of A. Pull the thread through.

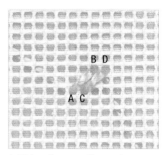

4 Take the needle to the back at D, one canvas thread to the right of B. Pull the thread through.

5 Stitching from left to right, work two more diagonal stitches in exactly the same manner.

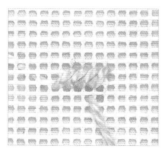

6 Bring the thread to the front, one canvas thread below the base of the previous stitch.

7 Take the needle to the back, one canvas thread below the tip of the previous stitch. Pull the thread through.

8 Stitching downwards, work two more diagonal stitches in exactly the same manner.

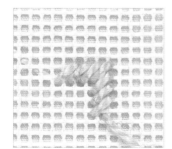

9 Bring the thread to the front, one canvas thread to the right of the base of the previous stitch.

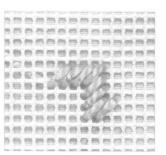

10 Take the needle to the back, one canvas thread to the right of the tip of the previous stitch and pull through.

11 Stitching from left to right, work two more diagonal stitches in exactly the same manner.

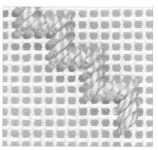

12 Working diagonally from left to right, continue working stitches across the row.

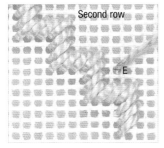

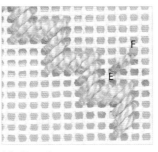

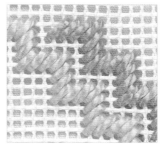

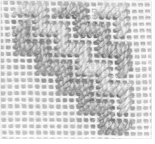

13 Bring the thread to the front one canvas intersection away from the tip of the stitch on the inside corner of the previous row (E).

14 Crossing two canvas intersections, take the needle to the back at F, diagonally upwards and to the right. Pull the thread through.

15 Working diagonally from right to left and keeping one canvas thread free between this row and the previous row, continue across the row.

16 Continue working rows of stitches back and forth across the canvas, keeping one canvas thread free between each row.

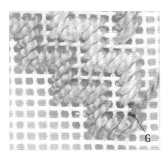

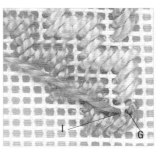

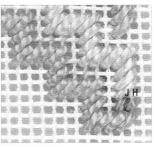

17 Secure a new thread on the lower right hand side. Bring it to the front at G, through the same hole as the tip of the second to last stitch along the bottom.

18 Crossing one canvas intersection, take the needle to the back at H, above and to the right. Pull the thread through.

19 Re-emerge at I, one canvas thread to the left of G. Pull the thread through.

20 Take the needle to the back at J, one canvas thread to the left of H. Pull the thread through.

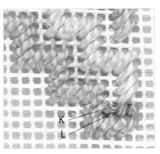

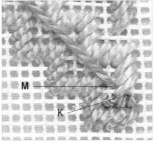

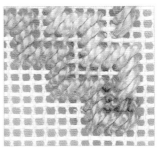

21 To begin the vertical stitches, bring the needle to the front at K, at the top of the stitch. This is one canvas thread to the left of J.

22 Take the needle to the back at L, one canvas intersection below and to the left of K. Pull the thread through.

23 Re-emerge at M, one canvas thread above K. Pull the thread through.

24 Work the next two stitches in the same manner, taking the thread from top right to bottom left each time.

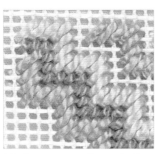

25 Bring the thread to the front at N, in the bottom left corner of the next stitch.

26 Continue to the end of the row, repeating the sequence of three horizontal stitches from bottom left to top right and three vertical stitches from top right to bottom left.

27 Turn the canvas upside down. Bring the thread to the front in the same manner as the first row.

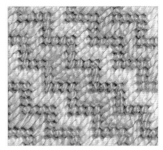

28 Continue working rows of stitches in the same manner as before, turning the canvas after each one.

Berlin work

This form of needlepoint originated in Germany in the 19th century. The first charts were released in 1804 by a print seller named Philipson who began publishing needlework designs on graph paper. Within the next forty years, at least 14,000 different designs were produced.

In 1810, another Berlin print seller, named Wittich, began selling Berlin work charts. He also hired artists to create charts of classic and popular paintings. Each square on a chart was hand coloured to indicate the required thread colour. Colourful bouquets, wreaths and baskets of naturalistic flowers along with Shakespearian and biblical scenes, romantic landscapes and whimsical pets were common subjects.

Tent and cross stitches were the most commonly used stitches. One particular variation, often known as raised Berlin work or plush work, used areas of velvet stitch among the tent and cross stitches. These areas were trimmed and shaped, giving the finished embroideries a sculpted appearance.

Another important characteristic of Berlin work was the type and quality of wool used. The wool of Zephyr merinos was the most sought after. Zephyr wool took dye exceptionally well and readily allowed extremely brilliant colours. With time, it came to be produced in fifty different colour families with five shades within each family.

Virtually anyone could produce stunning embroideries and the popularity of Berlin work grew. From about 1830 to 1870 it was so prolific in Europe and America that it displaced almost every other form of embroidery. Every type of household item imaginable was decorated with Berlin work. These included such items as upholstery fabrics, bellpulls, cushions, valances, suspenders, slippers, vests, purses, firescreens, coverlets and the like.

KALEM STITCH

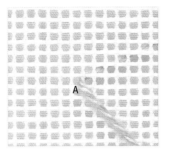

1 Secure the thread. Bring it to the front at A, on the upper right hand side.

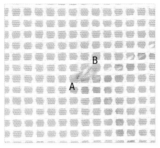

2 Take the needle to the back at B, one canvas thread above and two canvas threads to the right of A. Pull the thread through.

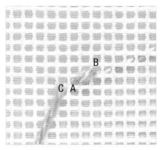

3 Re-emerge at C, one canvas thread to the left of A. Pull the thread through.

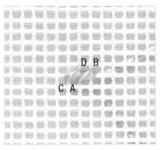

4 Take the needle to the back at D, one canvas thread to the left of B. Pull the thread through.

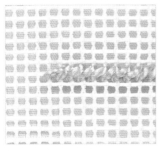

5 Continue working stitches from right to left across the row in the same manner.

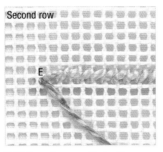

6 Bring the needle to the front through the same hole as the lower end of the last stitch (E). Pull the thread through.

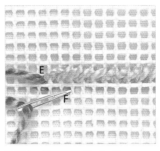

7 Take the needle to the back at F, one canvas thread below and two canvas threads to the right of E.

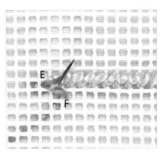

8 Pull the thread through. Re-emerge one canvas thread to the right of E.

9 Pull the thread through. Continue working stitches, from left to right, across the row in the same manner.

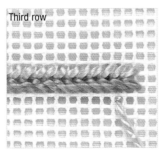

10 Bring the needle to the front two canvas threads below the upper end of the previous stitch. Pull the thread through.

11 Work stitches, from right to left, across the row in the same manner as before.

12 Continue working rows of stitches, back and forth, across the canvas.

KNITTING STITCH

This stitch must be worked on double or Penelope canvas.

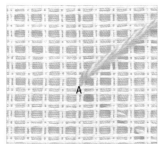

1 Secure the thread. Bring it to the front at A, between a pair of canvas threads on the lower right hand side.

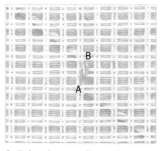

2 Take the needle to the back at B, just to the right of the pair of threads and one pair of threads above A. Pull the thread through.

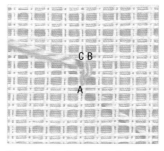

3 To begin the second stitch, bring the needle to the front at C, one pair of canvas threads directly above A. Pull the thread through.

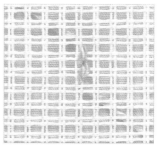

4 Work the second stitch following step 2.

5 Continue working stitches up the row in the same manner.

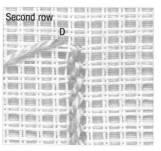

6 Bring the needle to the front one pair of canvas threads to the left of the top of the last stitch (D). Pull the thread through.

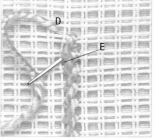

7 Keeping the thread on the left hand side, take the needle to the back at E, the same hole as the base of the previous stitch.

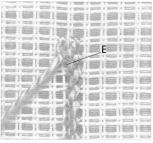

8 Pull the thread through. Re-emerge one canvas thread to the left of E and pull the thread through.

9 Continue working stitches down the row in the same manner.

10 Bring the needle to the front between the next pair of canvas threads to the left. Pull the thread through.

11 Work stitches up the row in the same manner as before.

12 Continue working rows of stitches up and down the canvas.

KNOTTED STITCH

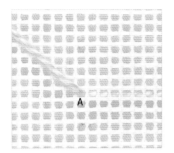

1 Secure the thread. Bring it to the front at A, on the upper right hand side.

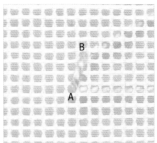

2 Take the needle to the back at B, three canvas threads above and one canvas thread to the right of A. Pull the thread through.

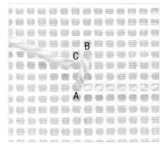

3 Re-emerge at C, one canvas intersection below and to the left of B. Pull the thread through.

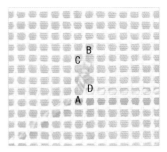

4 Take the needle over the previous stitch and to the back at D, one canvas intersection below and to the right of C. Pull the thread through.

5 To begin the second stitch, bring the needle to the front at E, one canvas thread to the left of A. Pull the thread through.

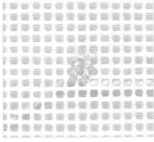

6 Work the second stitch following steps 2–4.

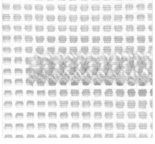

7 Continue working stitches, from right to left, across the row in the same manner.

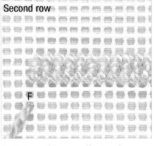

8 Bring the needle to the front two canvas threads below the lower end of the last stitch (F). Pull the thread through.

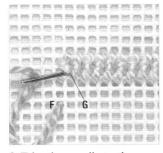

9 Take the needle to the back at G, three canvas threads above and one to the right of F. This is between the last and second to last stitches of the previous row.

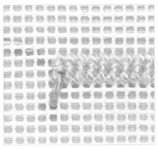

10 Pull the thread through.

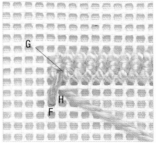

11 Re-emerge at H, two canvas threads directly below G and pull the thread through.

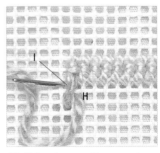

12 Take the needle over the previous stitch and to the back at I, one canvas intersection above and to the left of H.

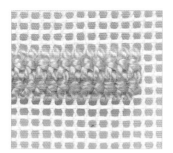

13 Pull the thread through. Continue working stitches, from left to right, across the row in the same manner.

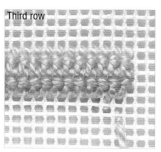

14 Bring the needle to the front two canvas threads below the lower end of the last long stitch. Pull the thread through.

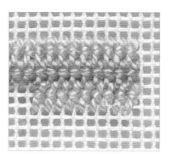

15 Work stitches, from right to left, across the row in the same manner as before.

16 Continue working rows of stitches, back and forth, across the canvas.

LEAF STITCH

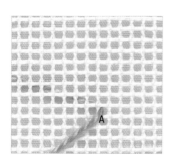

1 Secure the thread. Bring it to the front at A on the upper left hand side.

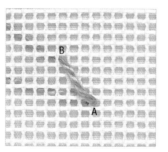

2 Take the needle to the back at B, three canvas threads to the left and four canvas threads above A. Pull the thread through.

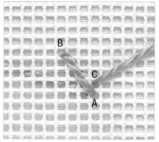

3 Re-emerge at C, one canvas thread above A. Pull the thread through.

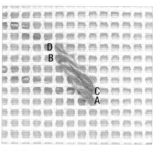

4 Take the needle to the back at D, one canvas thread above B. Pull the thread through.

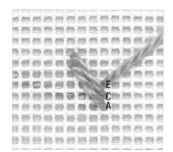

5 Re-emerge at E, one canvas thread above C. Pull the thread through.

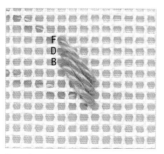

6 Take the needle to the back at F, one canvas thread above D. Pull the thread through.

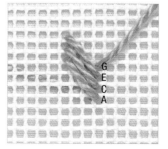

7 Re-emerge at G, one canvas thread above E. Pull the thread through.

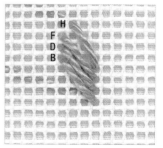

8 Take the needle to the back at H, one canvas intersection above and to the right of F. Pull the thread through.

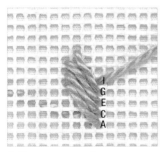

9 Re-emerge at I, one canvas thread above G. Pull the thread through.

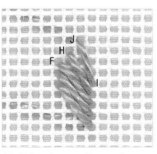

10 Take the needle to the back at J, one canvas intersection above and to the right of H. Pull the thread through.

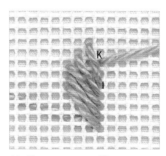

11 Re-emerge at K, two canvas threads above I. Pull the thread through.

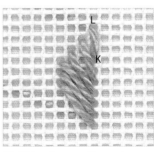

12 Take the needle to the back at L, three canvas threads above K. Pull the thread through.

13 Re-emerge at I again, taking care not to split the thread in the shared hole. Pull the thread through.

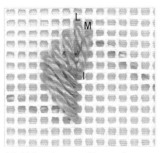

14 Take the needle to the back at M, one canvas intersection below and to the right of L. Pull the thread through.

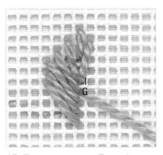

15 Re-emerge at G again, taking care not to split the thread in the shared hole. Pull the thread through.

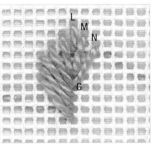

16 Take the needle to the back at N, one canvas intersection below and to the right of M. Pull the thread through.

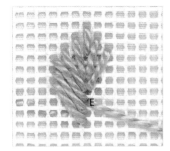

17 Re-emerge at E again, taking care not to split the thread in the shared hole. Pull the thread through.

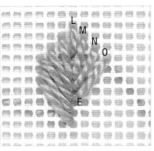

18 Take the needle to the back at O, one canvas intersection below and to the right of N. Pull the thread through.

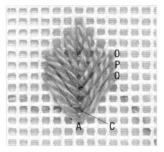

19 Work two more stitches in the same manner (C–P and A–Q).

20 To begin the second leaf stitch, bring the needle to the front at R, six canvas threads to the right of A. Pull the thread through.

21 Work the second stitch, following steps 2–19. Take care not to split the thread in the shared holes.

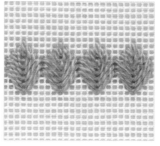

22 Continue working stitches across the row in the same manner.

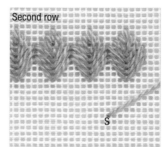

23 Bring the thread to the front at S, three canvas threads to the left and six below the lowest point of the previous stitch.

24 Take the needle to the back at T, four canvas threads above and three canvas threads to the right of S. Pull the thread through.

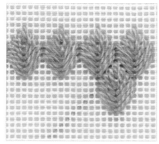

25 Reversing the order of the stitches, work this leaf stitch in a similar manner to before.

26 Continue working stitches, from right to left, across the row.

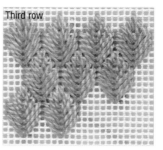

27 Work the third row in exactly the same manner as the first row.

28 Continue working rows of stitches back and forth across the canvas.

LEVIATHAN STITCH

Also known as double cross stitch, star eyelet stitch and smyrna stitch.

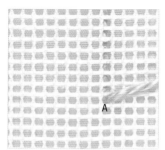

1 Secure the thread. Bring it to the front at A, on the upper left hand side. This is the lower right hand corner of the stitch.

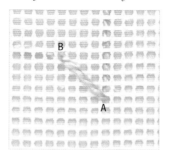

2 Crossing four canvas intersections, take the needle to the back at B. This is the upper left hand corner of the stitch. Pull the thread through.

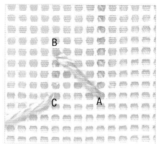

3 Re-emerge at C, four canvas threads below B. Pull the thread through.

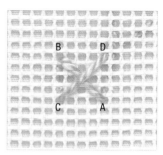

4 Crossing four canvas intersections, take the needle to the back at D in the upper right hand corner of the stitch. Pull the thread through.

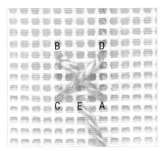

5 Re-emerge at E, halfway between A and C. Pull the thread through.

6 Crossing four canvas threads, take the needle to the back at F, directly above. Pull the thread through.

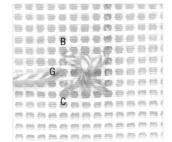

7 Re-emerge at G, halfway between B and C. Pull the thread through.

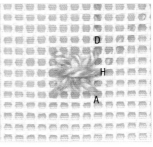

8 Crossing four canvas threads to the right, take the needle to the back at H. Pull the thread through.

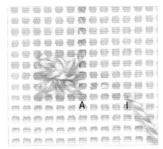

9 To begin the second leviathan stitch, bring the needle to the front at I, four canvas threads to the right of A.

10 Work the second stitch, following steps 2–8. Take care not to split the thread in the shared holes on the left hand side.

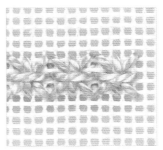

11 Continue working stitches across the row in the same manner.

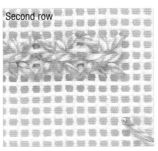

12 Bring the needle to the front four canvas threads below the lower right hand corner of the last stitch. Pull the thread through.

13 Work the stitch following steps 2–8. Take care not to split the thread in the shared holes on the upper side.

14 To begin the second stitch of this row, bring the needle to the front through the same hole as the lower left hand corner of the previous stitch. Pull the thread through.

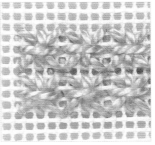

15 Complete the row in the same manner as before.

16 Continue working rows of stitches, back and forth, across the canvas.

LEVIATHAN STITCH – DOUBLE

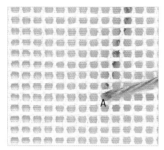

1 Secure the thread. Bring it to the front at A, on the upper left hand side. This is the lower right hand corner of the stitch.

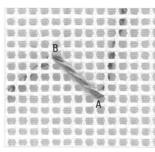

2 Crossing four canvas intersections, take the needle to the back at B in the upper left hand corner. Pull the thread through.

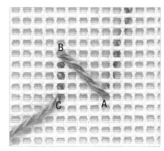

3 Re-emerge at C, four canvas threads below B. Pull the thread through.

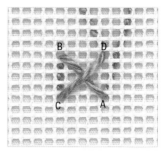

4 Crossing four canvas intersections, take the needle to the back at D in the upper right hand corner of the stitch. Pull the thread through.

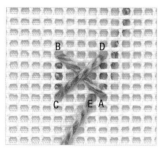

5 Re-emerge at E, one canvas thread to the left of A. Pull the thread through.

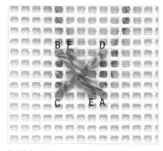

6 Take the needle to the back at F, one canvas thread to the right of B. Pull the thread through.

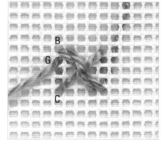

7 Re-emerge at G, one canvas thread below B. Pull the thread through.

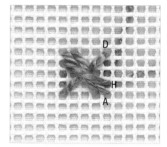

8 Take the needle to the back at H, one canvas thread above A. Pull the thread through.

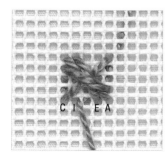

9 Re-emerge at I, one canvas thread to the right of C. Pull the thread through.

10 Take the needle to the back at J, one canvas thread to the left of D. Pull the thread through.

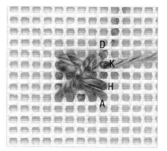

11 Re-emerge at K, one canvas thread below D. Pull the thread through.

12 Take the needle to the back at L, one canvas thread above C. Pull the thread through.

LEVIATHAN STITCH – DOUBLE

13 Re-emerge at M, one canvas thread to the right of I. Pull the thread through.

14 Take the needle to the back at N, one canvas thread to the right of F. Pull the thread through.

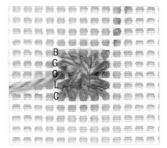

15 Re-emerge at O, one canvas thread below G. Pull the thread through.

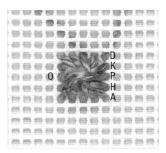

16 Take the needle to the back at P, one canvas thread below K. Pull the thread through.

17 To begin the second stitch, bring the needle to the front at Q, four canvas threads to the right of A. Pull the thread through.

18 Work the second stitch, following steps 2–16. Take care not to split the thread in the shared holes on the left hand side.

19 Continue working stitches across the row in the same manner.

20 Bring the needle to the front four canvas threads below the lower right hand corner of the last stitch.

21 Work the stitch following steps 2–16. Take care not to split the thread in the shared holes on the upper side.

22 To begin the second stitch of this row, bring the needle to the front through the same hole as the lower left hand corner of the previous stitch. Pull the thread through.

23 Complete the row, from right to left, in the same manner as before.

24 Continue working rows of stitches, back and forth, across the canvas.

MILANESE STITCH

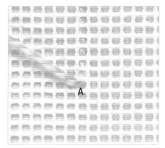

1 Secure the thread. Bring it to the front at A on the upper left hand side.

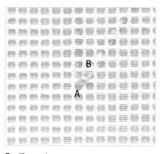

2 Crossing one canvas intersection, take the needle to the back at B above and to the right of A. Pull the thread through.

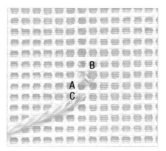

3 Re-emerge at C, one canvas thread below A. Pull the thread through.

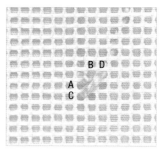

4 Take the needle to the back at D, one canvas thread to the right of B. Pull the thread through.

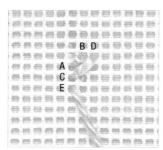

5 Re-emerge at E, one canvas thread below C. Pull the thread through.

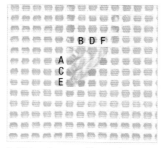

6 Take the needle to the back at F, one canvas thread to the right of D. Pull the thread through.

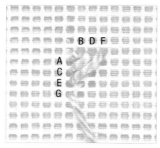

7 Re-emerge at G, one canvas thread below E. Pull the thread through.

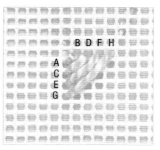

8 Take the needle to the back at H, one canvas thread to the right of F. Pull the thread through.

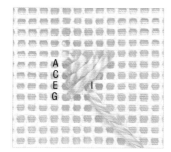

9 To begin the second stitch, bring the needle to the front at I, two canvas threads to the right of E. Pull the thread through.

10 Work the second stitch, following steps 2–8.

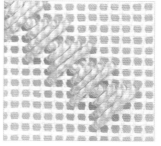

11 Continue working stitches diagonally across the row in the same manner.

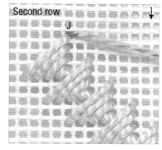

12 Turn the canvas upside down. Bring the needle to the front at J, through the same hole as the tip of the last stitch. Pull the thread through.

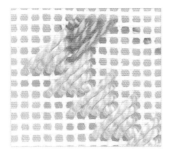

13 Work the stitch following steps 2–8.

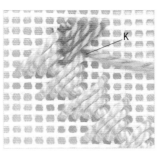

14 For the second stitch, bring the needle to the front at K. Pull the thread through.

15 Continue working stitches diagonally, from left to right, across the row in the same manner as before.

16 Continue working rows of stitches, turning the canvas after each one.

MOSAIC STITCH

1 Secure the thread. Bring it to the front at A, on the upper right hand side.

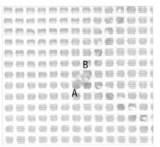

2 Crossing one canvas intersection, take the needle to the back at B, above and to the right of A. Pull the thread through.

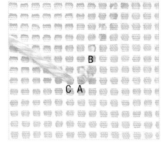

3 Re-emerge at C, one canvas thread to the left of A. Pull the thread through.

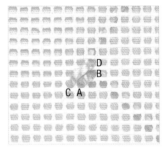

4 Crossing two canvas intersections, take the needle to the back at D, one canvas thread above B. Pull the thread through.

5 Re-emerge at E, one canvas thread above C. Pull the thread through.

6 Crossing one canvas intersection, take the needle to the back at F, one canvas thread to the left of D. Pull the thread through.

7 To begin the second mosaic stitch, bring the needle to the front at G, one canvas thread to the left of C. Pull the thread through.

8 Work the second stitch, following steps 2–6. Take care not to split the thread in the shared hole on the right hand side.

81

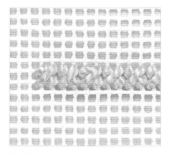

9 Continue working stitches, from right to left, across the row in the same manner.

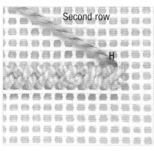

10 Turn the canvas upside down. Bring the thread to the front at H, through the shared hole at the top left of the previous stitch.

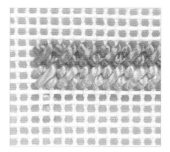

11 Work the stitch following steps 2–6. Continue across the row in the same manner.

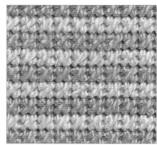

12 Continue working rows of stitches, turning the canvas after each row.

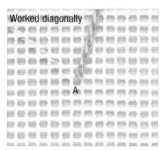

1 Secure the thread. Bring it to the front at A, on the upper left hand side.

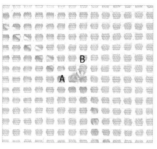

2 Crossing one canvas intersection, take the needle to the back at B, above and to the right of A. Pull the thread through.

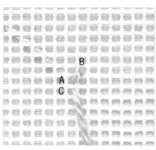

3 Re-emerge at C, one canvas thread below A. Pull the thread through.

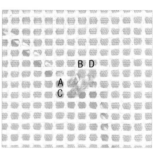

4 Crossing two canvas intersections, take the needle to the back at D, one canvas thread to the right of B. Pull the thread through.

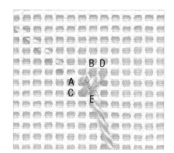

5 Re-emerge at E, one canvas thread to the right of C. Pull the thread through.

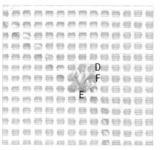

6 Crossing one canvas intersection, take the needle to the back at F, one canvas thread below D. Pull the thread through.

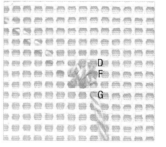

7 To begin the second mosaic stitch, bring the needle to the front at G, two canvas threads directly below F. Pull the thread through.

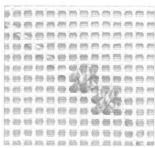

8 Work the second stitch, following steps 2–6.

MOSAIC STITCH / CONTINUED

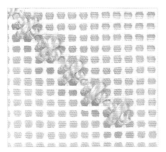

9 Continue working stitches, diagonally from left to right, across the row in the same manner.

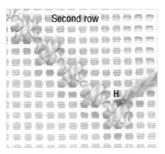

10 Bring the needle to the front at H, through the same hole at the top left of the previous stitch. Pull the thread through.

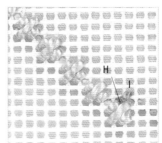

11 Take the needle to the back at I, one canvas intersection above and to the right of H. Pull the thread through.

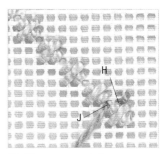

12 Re-emerge at J, one canvas thread to the left of H. Pull the thread through.

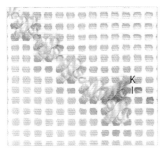

13 Crossing two canvas intersections, take the needle to the back at K, one canvas thread above I. Pull the thread through.

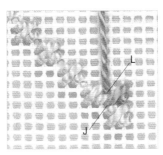

14 Re-emerge at L, one canvas thread above J. Pull the thread through.

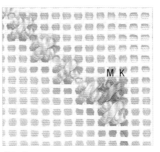

15 Crossing one canvas intersection, take the needle to the back at M, one canvas thread to the left of K. Pull the thread through.

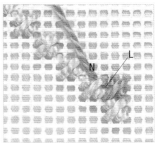

16 To begin the second mosaic stitch, bring the needle to the front at N, one canvas intersection above and to the left of L. Pull the thread through.

17 Work this stitch, following steps 11–15.

18 Continue across the row in the same manner.

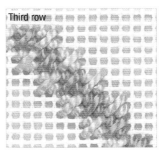

19 Work the third row in exactly the same manner as the first row.

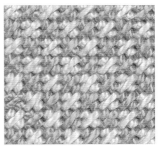

20 Continue working rows of stitches diagonally back and forth across the canvas.

ORIENTAL STITCH

Oriental stitch is a variation of Milanese stitch.

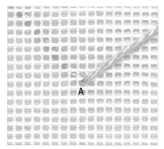

1 Secure the thread. Bring it to the front at A on the upper left hand side.

2 Work the first row following steps 2–11 of Milanese stitch on page 80.

3 Turn the canvas upside down. Bring the needle to the front at B, four canvas threads to the right and one canvas thread below the tip of the last stitch. Pull the thread through.

4 Work the stitch following steps 2–8 on page 80. The longest stitch of this sequence aligns with the longest stitch of the third to last sequence in the previous row.

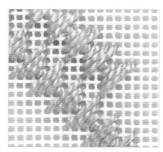

5 Continue working stitches diagonally across the row in the same manner.

6 Continue working rows of stitches in the same manner, turning the canvas after each one.

7 Using a new thread, bring it to the front at C, one canvas thread below the lower left hand corner of the first Milanese stitch.

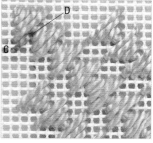

8 Crossing two canvas intersections, take the needle to the back at D, above and to the right of C. Pull the thread through.

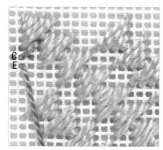

9 Re-emerge at E, one canvas thread below C. Pull the thread through.

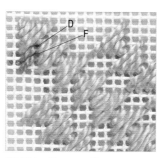

10 Take the needle to the back at F, one canvas thread below D. Pull the thread through.

11 Re-emerge at G, one canvas thread below E. Pull the thread through.

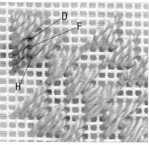

12 Take the needle to the back at H, one canvas thread below F. Pull the thread through.

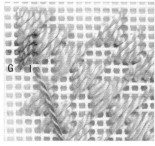

13 To begin the second stitch, bring the needle to the front at I, two canvas threads to the left of G.

14 Work the second stitch, following steps 8–12. Take care not to split the thread in the shared holes.

15 Continue working stitches diagonally across the row in the same manner.

16 Bring the needle to the front at J, one canvas thread to the left of the lower left hand corner of the last Milanese stitch of the next row. Pull the thread through.

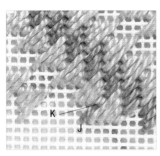

17 Crossing two canvas intersections, take the needle to the back at K, above and to the right of J. Pull the thread through.

18 Re-emerge at L, one canvas thread to the left of J. Pull the thread through.

19 Take the needle to the back at M, one canvas thread to the left of K. Pull the thread through.

20 Re-emerge at N, one canvas to the left of L. Pull the thread through.

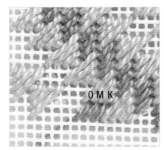

21 Take the needle to the back at O, one canvas thread to the left of M. Pull the thread through.

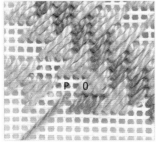

22 To begin the second stitch of this row, bring the needle to the front at P, two canvas threads to the left of O. Pull the thread through.

23 Complete the stitch in the same manner as before and continue working stitches diagonally up the row.

24 Continue working rows of stitches, diagonally back and forth, across the canvas.

PARISIAN STITCH

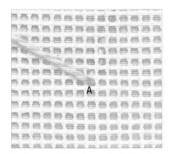

1 Secure the thread. Bring it to the front at A, on the upper right hand side.

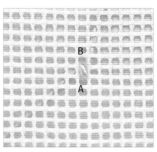

2 Take the needle to the back at B, two canvas threads above A. Pull the thread through.

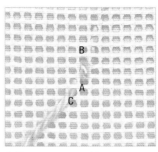

3 Re-emerge at C, one canvas intersection below and to the left of A. Pull the thread through.

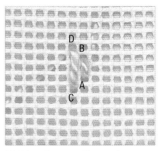

4 Take the needle to the back at D, four canvas threads above C. Pull the thread through.

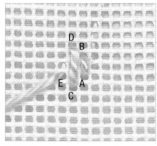

5 To begin the second stitch, bring the needle to the front at E, one canvas intersection above and to the left of C. Pull the thread through.

6 Work the second stitch following steps 2–4.

7 Continue working stitches, from right to left, across the row in the same manner.

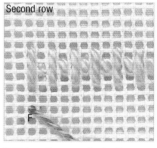

8 Bring the needle to the front two canvas threads below the lower end of the last stitch (F). Pull the thread through.

9 Take the needle to the back at G, two canvas threads above F. Pull the thread through. This is the same hole as the end of the last stitch of the previous row.

10 Re-emerge at H, one canvas intersection below and to the right of F. Pull the thread through.

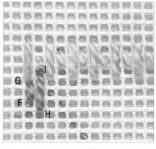

11 Take the needle to the back at I, four canvas threads above H. Pull the thread through. This is the same hole as the end of the second to last stitch of the previous row.

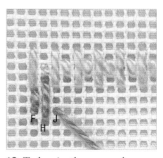

12 To begin the second stitch of this row, bring the needle to the front at J, one canvas intersection above and to the right of H. Pull the thread through.

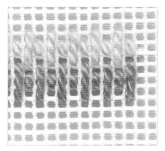

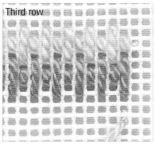

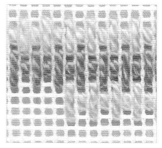

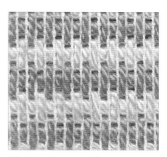

13 Continue working stitches, from left to right, across the row in the same manner.

14 Bring the needle to the front two canvas threads below the lower end of the last stitch. Pull the thread through.

15 Work stitches, from right to left, across the row in the same manner as before.

16 Continue working rows of stitches back and forth across the canvas.

PERSPECTIVE STITCH

Four rows of stitches are used to create one row of Perspective stitch.

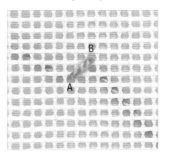

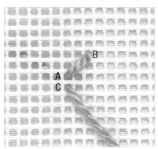

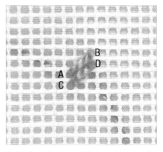

1 Secure the thread. Bring it to the front at A, on the upper left hand side.

2 Take the needle to the back at B, two canvas intersections above and to the right of A. Pull the thread through.

3 Re-emerge at C, one canvas thread below A. Pull the thread through.

4 Take the needle to the back at D, one canvas thread below B. Pull the thread through.

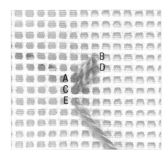

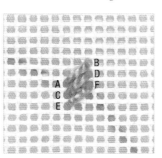

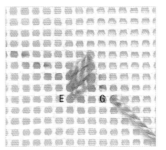

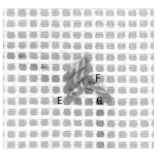

5 Re-emerge at E, one canvas thread below C. Pull the thread through.

6 Take the needle to the back at F, one canvas thread below D. Pull the thread through.

7 Re-emerge at G, four canvas threads to the right of E. Pull the thread through.

8 Take the needle to the back at F, taking care not to split the thread in the shared hole. Pull the thread through.

PERSPECTIVE STITCH / CONTINUED

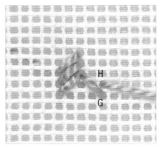

9 Re-emerge at H, one canvas thread above G. Pull the thread through.

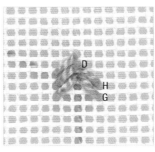

10 Take the needle to the back at D, taking care not to split the thread in the shared hole. Pull the thread through.

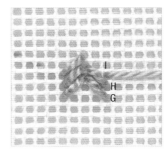

11 Re-emerge at I, one canvas thread above H. Pull the thread through.

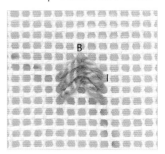

12 Take the needle to the back at B, taking care not to split the thread in the shared hole. Pull the thread through.

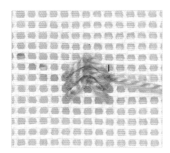

13 To begin the second sequence of stitches, bring the needle to the front at I again. Pull the thread through.

14 Work the second sequence following steps 2–12.

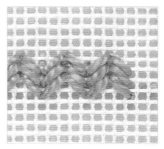

15 Continue working stitches, from left to right across the row, in the same manner.

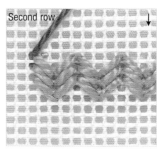

16 Turn the canvas upside down. Bring the needle to the front through the same hole as the tip of the last stitch. Pull the thread through.

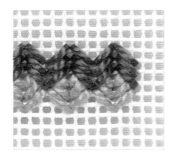

17 Work the row in exactly the same manner as the first row, partially overlapping the stitches of the first row.

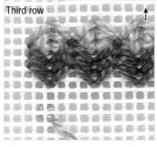

18 Turn the canvas upside down. Bring the needle to the front three canvas threads below the base of the last stitch of the previous row. Pull the thread through.

19 Crossing two canvas intersections, take the needle to the back, above and to the left. Pull the thread through.

20 Work two more stitches in the same manner directly above the first stitch.

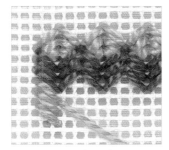

21 Bring the thread to the front through the same hole as the base of the last worked stitch.

22 Repeating steps 2–12, work stitches from left to right across the row.

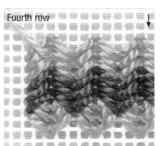

23 Turn the canvas upside down. Bring the needle to the front two canvas threads below the tip of the last stitch.

24 Pull the thread through. Repeat steps 19–21.

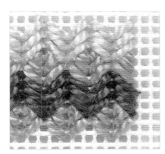

25 Repeating steps 2–12, work stitches from left to right across the row.

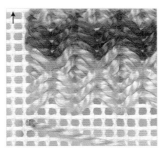

26 To repeat the sequence, turn the canvas upside down. Bring the thread to the front one canvas thread below the base of the previous stitch.

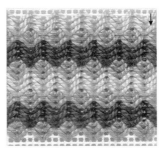

27 Repeat the sequence of four rows, turning the canvas after each row.

28 Continue working rows of stitches in the same manner, turning the canvas after each one.

QUICK STITCH

It is important to ensure the laid stitches accurately align with the canvas intersections.

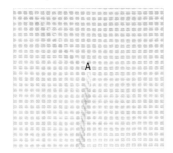

1 Secure the thread. Bring it to the front at A, on the upper left hand side.

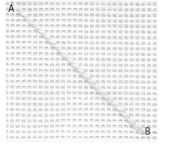

2 Take the needle to the back at B, on the lower right hand side, ensuring the thread aligns with the canvas intersections. Pull the thread through.

3 Re-emerge at C, two canvas threads above B. Pull the thread through.

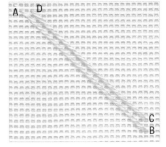

4 Take the needle to the back at D, two canvas threads to the right of A. Pull the thread through.

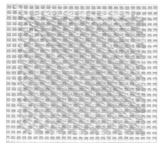

5 Continue laying threads, back and forth across the canvas in the same manner. Repeat the procedure below the first laid thread.

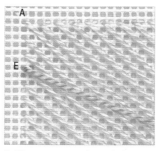

6 Using a new thread, bring it to the front at E, six canvas threads below A. Pull the thread through.

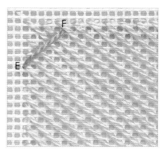

7 Crossing four laid threads, take the needle to the back at F, five canvas intersections above and to the right of E. Pull the thread through.

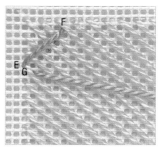

8 Keeping to the right of the laid thread, re-emerge at G, one canvas intersection below and to the right of E.

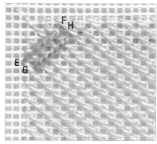

9 Crossing four laid threads, take the needle to the back at H, five canvas intersections above and to the right of G. Pull the thread through.

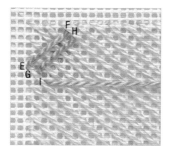

10 Keeping to the right of the laid thread, re-emerge at I, one canvas intersection below and to the right of G.

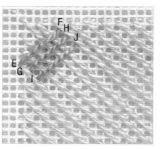

11 Crossing four laid threads, take the needle to the back at J, five canvas intersections above and to the right of I. Pull the thread through.

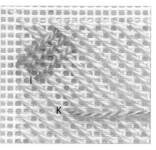

12 To begin the second set of stitches, bring the thread to the front at K, four canvas intersections below and to the right of I. Ensure it is to the right of the laid thread.

13 Work a second set of stitches following steps 7–11.

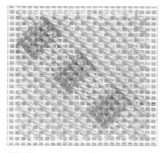

14 Continue in this manner, covering the same four laid threads, to the end of the row.

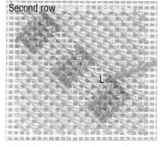

15 Bring the needle to the front at L, two canvas threads to the left of the upper corner of the last block of stitches. Pull the thread through.

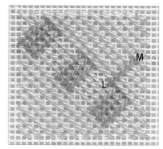

16 Crossing four laid threads, take the needle to the back at M, five canvas intersections above and to the right of L. Pull the thread through.

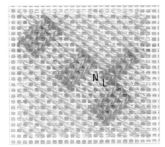

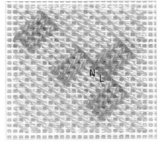

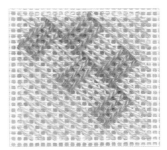

17 Re-emerging at N, one canvas intersection above and to the left of L, work a second stitch in the same manner as the first.

18 Re-emerging one canvas intersection above and to the left of N, work a third stitch in the same manner as the first.

19 Continue working stitches, diagonally up the row in the same manner.

20 Continue working diagonal rows of stitches back and forth across the canvas.

RAY STITCH

Ray stitch is also known as fan stitch.

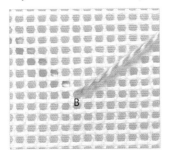

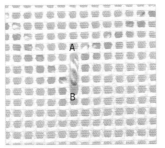

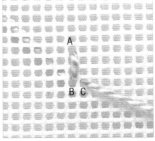

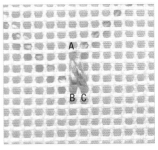

1 Secure the thread. Bring it to the front at B, on the upper left hand side.

2 Take the needle to the back at A, three canvas threads above B. Pull the thread through.

3 Re-emerge at C, one canvas thread to the right of B. Pull the thread through.

4 Take the needle to the back at A again. Pull the thread through.

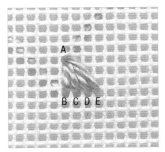

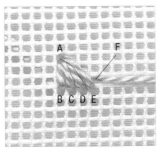

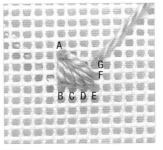

5 Moving one canvas thread to the right each time, work two more stitches in the same manner (D–A and E–A).

6 Re-emerge at F, one canvas thread above E. Pull the thread through.

7 Take the needle to the back at A again. Pull the thread through.

8 Re-emerge at G, one canvas thread above F. Pull the thread through.

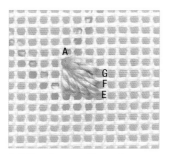

9 Take the needle to the back at A again. Pull the thread through.

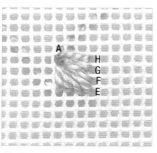

10 Starting one canvas thread above, work one more stitch in the same manner (H–A).

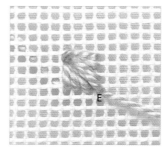

11 To begin the second stitch, bring the needle to the front at E. Pull the thread through.

12 Work the second stitch following steps 2–10.

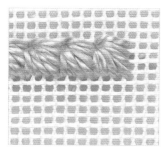

13 Continue working stitches, from left to right across the row, in the same manner.

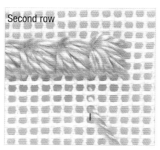

14 Bring the needle to the front at I, three canvas threads below the lower left hand corner of the last stitch. Pull the thread through.

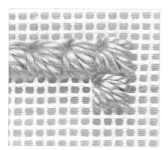

15 Work this stitch following steps 2–10.

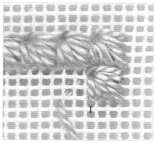

16 To begin the second stitch of this row, bring the needle to the front three canvas threads to the left of I. Pull the thread through.

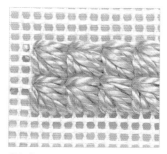

17 Continue working stitches, from right to left across the row, in the same manner.

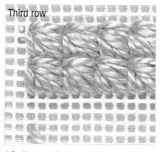

18 Bring the needle to the front three canvas threads below the lower left hand corner of the last stitch. Pull the thread through.

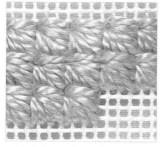

19 Work stitches, from left to right, across the row in the same manner as before.

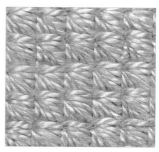

20 Continue working rows of stitches, back and forth, across the canvas.

RAY STITCH – EXPANDED

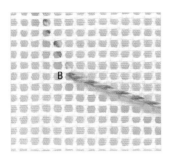

1 Secure the thread. Bring it to the front at B, on the upper left hand side.

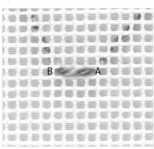

2 Take the needle to the back at A, three canvas threads to the right of B. Pull the thread through.

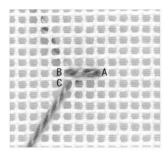

3 Re-emerge at C, one canvas thread below B. Pull the thread through.

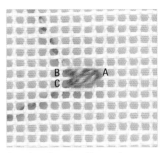

4 Take the needle to the back at A again. Pull the thread through.

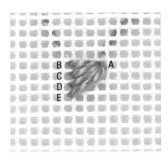

5 Moving one canvas thread below each time, work two more stitches in the same manner (D–A and E–A).

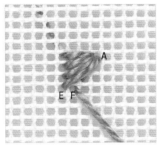

6 Bring the thread to the front at F, one canvas thread to the right of E. Pull the thread through.

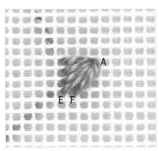

7 Take the needle to the back at A again. Pull the thread through.

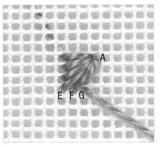

8 Re-emerge at G, one canvas thread to the right of F. Pull the thread through.

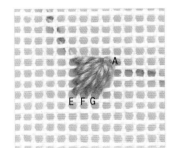

9 Take the needle to the back at A again. Pull the thread through.

10 Starting one canvas thread to the right each time, work four more stitches in the same manner (H–A, I–A, J–A and K–A).

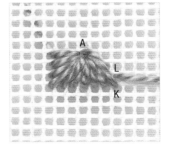

11 Bring the thread to the front at L, one canvas thread above K. Pull the thread through.

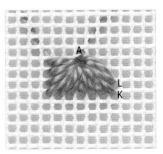

12 Take the needle to the back at A again. Pull the thread through.

13 Starting one canvas thread above each time, work two more stitches in the same manner (M–A and N–A).

14 To begin the second stitch, bring the needle to the front at N. Pull the thread through.

15 Work the second stitch following steps 2–13.

16 Continue working stitches, from left to right across the row, in the same manner.

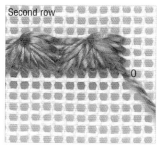

17 Bring the needle to the front at O, the lower right hand corner of the last stitch. Pull the thread through.

18 Reversing the order, work this stitch following steps 2–13.

19 To begin the second stitch of this row, bring the needle to the front six canvas threads to the left of O. Pull the thread through.

20 Continue working stitches, from right to left across the row, in the same manner.

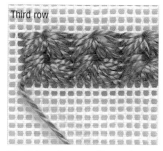

21 Bring the needle to the front at the lower left hand corner of the last stitch. Pull the thread through.

22 Work stitches, from left to right across the row, in the same manner as before.

23 Continue working rows of stitches, back and forth, across the canvas.

Firescreen, 18th century

RENAISSANCE STITCH

Renaissance stitches are always worked in blocks of four vertical stitches.

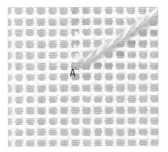

1 Secure the thread. Bring it to the front at A, on the upper right hand side.

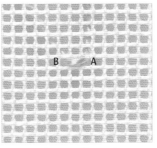

2 Take the needle to the back at B, two canvas threads to the left of A. Pull the thread through.

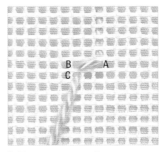

3 Re-emerge at C, one canvas thread below B. Pull the thread through.

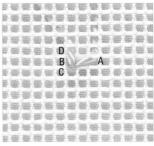

4 Take the needle to the back at D, one canvas thread above B. Pull the thread through.

5 Re-emerge at E, one canvas thread to the right of C. Pull the thread through.

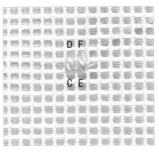

6 Take the needle to the back at F, two canvas threads above E. Pull the thread through.

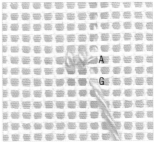

7 Re-emerge at G, two canvas threads below A. Pull the thread through.

8 Repeat steps 2–6.

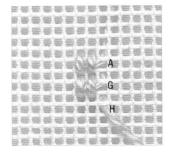

9 To begin the second block of stitches, bring the thread to the front at H, two canvas threads below G. Pull the thread through.

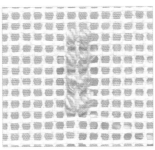

10 Work the block of stitches following steps 2–8.

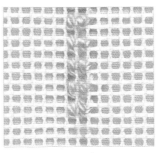

11 Continue working stitches down the row in the same manner.

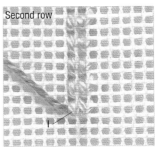

12 Bring the needle to the front at I, through the same hole as the left hand end of the last horizontal stitch. Pull the thread through.

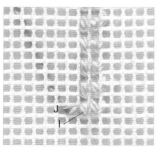

13 Take the needle to the back at J, two canvas threads to the left of I. Pull the thread through.

14 Work two vertical stitches over the horizontal stitch in the same manner as before.

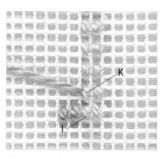

15 Bring the thread to the front at K, two canvas threads above I, to begin the second horizontal stitch.

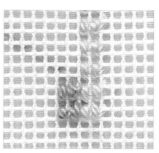

16 Work the horizontal stitch and two vertical stitches in the same manner as before.

17 Continue working stitches up the row in the same manner.

18 Bring the needle to the front through the same hole as the left hand end of the last horizontal stitch worked. Pull the thread through.

Rozashi

Rozashi is a little known traditional Japanese embroidery technique. It is believed to have its beginnings in the Nara period of this country's history (619–960AD). Rozashi was worked by the courtesans of the royal courts and was most favoured during the Edo and Meiji Periods.

The 'Ro' or canvas is made of finely woven silk with three interlocking weft threads to every warp thread. Stitches similar to brick, gobelin and Florentine stitch are worked with a highly twisted silk thread. The technique utilizes traditional Japanese patterns and symbols as the design elements. It is often used as appliqués for kimonos and obis, framed pictures, small purses, belts and other accessories that enhance clothing.

19 Work stitches down the row in the same manner as before.

20 Continue working rows of stitches up and down the canvas.

RHODES STITCH

Rhodes stitch can be worked over any number of canvas threads greater than three. Here, each stitch covers five vertical and five horizontal canvas threads.

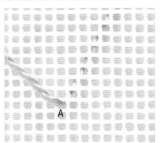

1 Secure the thread. Bring it to the front at A. This is one thread to the right of the lower left hand corner of the first stitch.

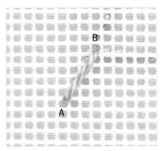

2 Take the needle to the back at B, five canvas threads above and three canvas threads to the right of A. Pull the thread through.

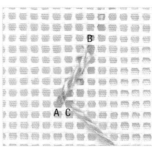

3 Re-emerge at C, one canvas thread to the right of A. Pull the thread through.

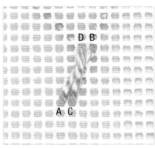

4 Take the needle to the back at D, one canvas thread to the left of B. Pull the thread through.

5 Re-emerge at E, one canvas thread to the right of C. Pull the thread through.

6 Take the needle to the back at F, one canvas thread to the left of D. Pull the thread through.

7 Re-emerge at G, one canvas thread to the right of E. Take the needle to the back at H, one canvas thread to the left of F. Pull the thread through.

8 Re-emerge at I, one canvas thread to the right of G. Pull the thread through.

9 Take the needle to the back at J, one canvas thread to the left of H. Pull the thread through.

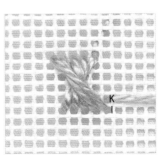

10 Re-emerge at K, one canvas thread above I. Pull the thread through.

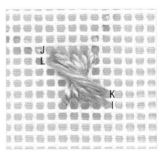

11 Take the needle to the back at L, one canvas thread below J. Pull the thread through.

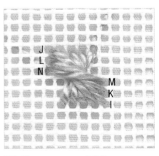

12 Re-emerge at M, one canvas thread above K. Take the needle to the back at N, one canvas thread below L. Pull the thread through.

13 Re-emerge at O, one canvas thread above M. Take the needle to the back at P, one canvas thread below N. Pull the thread through.

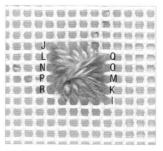

14 Re-emerge at Q, one canvas thread above O. Take the needle to the back at R, one canvas thread below P. Pull the thread through.

15 Re-emerge at S, one canvas thread above Q. Pull the thread through. This is the upper right hand corner of the stitch.

16 Take the needle to the back at T, one canvas thread below R. Pull the thread through. This is the lower left hand corner of the stitch.

17 To begin the second Rhodes stitch, bring the thread to the front at U, four canvas threads to the left of T. Pull the thread through.

18 Work the second stitch following steps 2–16.

19 Continue working stitches from right to left across the row in the same manner.

20 Bring the needle to the front five canvas threads below and one canvas thread to the right of the lower left hand corner of the last stitch. Pull the thread through.

21 Work stitches, from left to right across the row, in the same manner as before.

22 Bring the thread to the front five canvas threads below and one canvas thread to the right of the lower left hand corner of the last stitch. Pull the thread through.

23 Work the third row in exactly the same manner as the first row.

24 Continue working rows of stitches, back and forth, across the canvas.

RHODES STITCH – HALF

This stitch can be worked over any even number of canvas threads greater than three. Here, each stitch covers four vertical and four horizontal canvas threads.

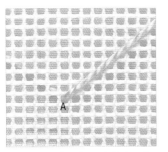

1 Secure the thread. Bring it to the front at A, on the upper left hand side. This is the lower left hand corner of the first stitch.

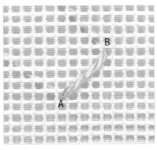

2 Take the needle to the back at B, four canvas threads above and four canvas threads to the right of A. Pull the thread through.

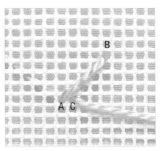

3 Re-emerge at C, one canvas thread to the right of A. Pull the thread through.

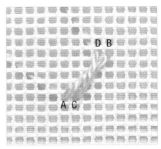

4 Take the needle to the back at D, one canvas thread to the left of B. Pull the thread through.

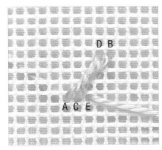

5 Re-emerge at E, one canvas thread to the right of C. Pull the thread through.

6 Take the needle to the back at F, one canvas thread to the left of D. Pull the thread through.

7 Re-emerge at G, one canvas thread to the right of E. Pull the thread through.

8 Take the needle to the back at H, one canvas thread to the left of F. Pull the thread through.

9 Re-emerge at I, one canvas thread to the right of G. Pull the thread through.

10 Take the needle to the back at J, one canvas thread to the left of H. Pull the thread through.

11 To begin the second stitch, bring the thread to the front at K, two canvas threads below G. Pull the thread through.

12 Work the second stitch following steps 2–10.

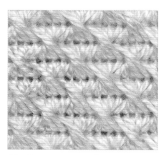

13 Continue working stitches diagonally, from left to right, down the canvas in the same manner.

14 Bring the thread to the front four canvas threads below the lower lefthand corner of the third to last stitch.

15 Work stitches, from right to left, diagonally up the canvas in the same manner as before.

16 Continue working diagonal rows of stitches, back and forth, across the canvas.

RICE STITCH

Also known as crossed corners and William and Mary stitch.

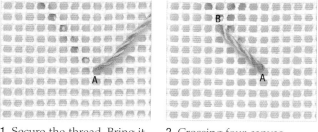

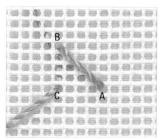

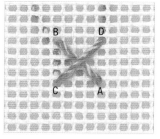

1 Secure the thread. Bring it to the front at A on the upper right hand side. This is the lower right hand corner of the stitch.

2 Crossing four canvas intersections, take the needle to the back at B, above and to the left. Pull the thread through.

3 Re-emerge at C, four canvas threads below B. Pull the thread through.

4 Crossing four canvas intersections, take the needle to the back at D above and to the right. Pull the thread through.

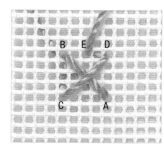

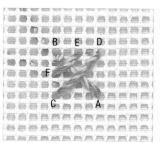

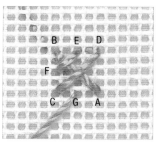

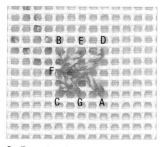

5 Bring the thread to the front at E, two canvas threads to the right of B. Pull the thread through.

6 Crossing two canvas intersections, take the needle to the back at F, below and to the left. Pull the thread through.

7 Re-emerge at G, two canvas threads to the left of A. Pull the thread through.

8 Crossing two canvas intersections, take the needle to the back at F, above and to the left. Pull the thread through.

RICE STITCH / CONTINUED

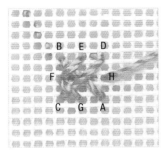

9 Re-emerge at H, two canvas threads above A. Pull the thread through.

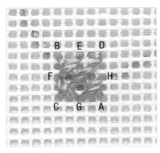

10 Crossing two canvas intersections, take the needle to the back at G, below and to the left. Pull the thread through.

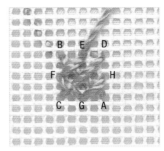

11 Re-emerge at E, two canvas threads to the right of B. Pull the thread through.

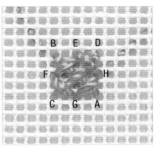

12 Crossing two canvas intersections, take the needle to the back at H, below and to the right. Pull the thread through.

13 To begin the second stitch, bring the needle to the front at C. Pull the thread through.

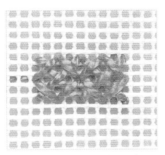

14 Work the second stitch, following steps 2–12. Take care not to split the thread in the shared holes on the right hand side.

15 Continue working stitches, from right to left, across the row in the same manner.

16 Bring the needle to the front four canvas threads below the lower right hand corner of the last stitch. Pull the thread through.

17 Work the stitch following steps 2–12. Take care not to split the thread in the shared holes on the upper side.

18 Continue working stitches, from left to right, across the row in the same manner.

19 Work the third row in exactly the same manner as the first row.

20 Continue working rows of stitches, back and forth, across the canvas.

ROCOCO STITCH

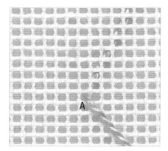

1 Secure the thread. Bring it to the front at A, on the upper right hand side.

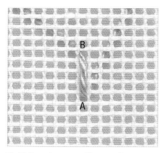

2 Take the needle to the back at B, four canvas threads above A. Pull the thread through.

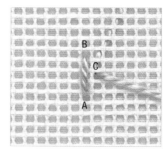

3 Re-emerge at C, two canvas threads above and one to the right of A. Pull the thread through.

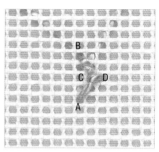

4 Slide the needle, from right to left, under the previous stitch, then take it to the back at D, one canvas thread to the right of C. Pull the thread through.

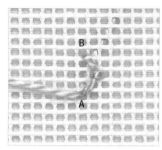

5 Re-emerge at A again. Pull the thread through.

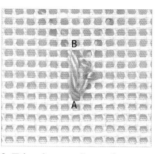

6 Take the needle to the back at B again. Pull the thread through.

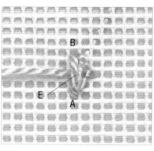

7 Re-emerge at E, one canvas thread to the left of C. Ensure the thread is to the left of the previous stitch. Pull the thread through.

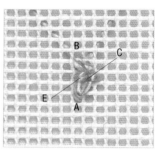

8 Take the needle to the back at C, one canvas thread to the right. Pull the thread through.

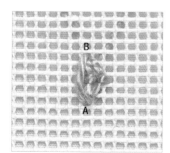

9 Work a third vertical stitch from A–B. Pull the thread through.

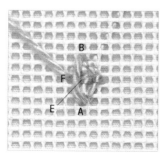

10 Re-emerge at F, one canvas thread to the left of E. Pull the thread through.

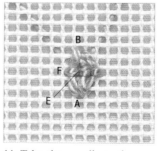

11 Take the needle to the back at E, one canvas thread to the right. Pull the thread through.

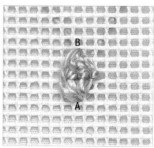

12 Work a fourth vertical stitch from A–B. Pull the thread through.

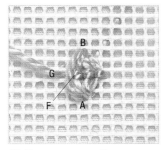

13 Re-emerge at G, one canvas thread to the left of F. Pull the thread through.

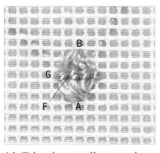

14 Take the needle over the vertical straight stitch and then to the back at F, one canvas thread to the right. Pull the thread through.

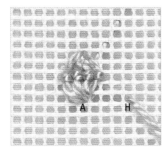

15 To begin the second stitch, bring the thread to the front at H, four canvas threads to the right of A. Pull the thread through.

16 Work the second stitch following steps 2–14.

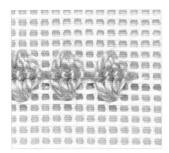

17 Continue working stitches, from left to right across the row, in the same manner.

18 Bring the needle to the front two canvas intersections below and to the left of the lower end of the last stitch (I). Pull the thread through.

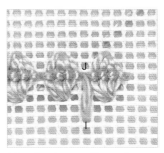

19 Take the needle to the back at J, four canvas threads above I. Pull the thread through. This is between the last and second to last stitches of the previous row.

20 Bring the thread to the front at K, one canvas thread to the right and two canvas threads above I. Pull the thread through.

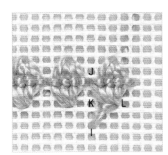

21 Slide the needle, from right to left, behind the vertical stitch, then take it to the back at L, one canvas thread to the right of K. Pull the thread through.

22 Working from right to left, work three more vertical stitches and anchor them with short horizontal stitches in the same manner as before.

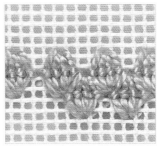

23 Continue working stitches, from right to left, across the row in the same manner.

24 Continue working rows of stitches, back and forth, across the canvas.

RYA STITCH

Rya stitch is also known as Ghiordes knot and Turkey work.

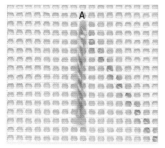

1 Leaving a tail of thread on the front, take the thread from front to back at the position for the first stitch (A).

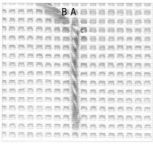

2 Holding the tail of thread, bring the needle to the front at B, one canvas thread to the left of A. Pull the thread through.

3 Take the needle to the back at C, one canvas thread to the right of A. Pull the thread through.

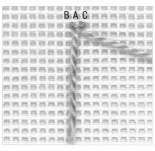

4 Re-emerge at A again. Pull the thread through.

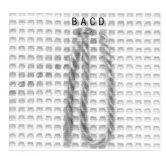

5 Take the needle to the back at D, one canvas thread to the right of C. Pull the thread through leaving a loop on the front.

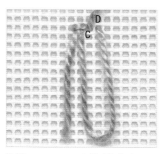

6 Re-emerge at C. Pull the thread through, taking care to maintain the loop.

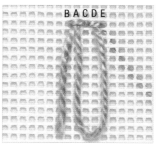

7 Take the needle to the back at E, one canvas thread to the right of D. Pull the thread through to form a straight stitch.

8 Re-emerge at D. Pull the thread through.

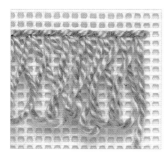

9 Continue working loops and straight stitches, from left to right, across the row in the same manner. Hold each loop as you work the next straight stitch.

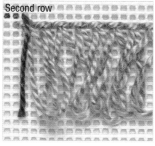

10 Return to the left hand side and take the needle to the back one canvas thread above A. Pull the thread through, leaving a tail.

11 Work stitches, from left to right, across the row in the same manner as before.

12 Continue working rows of stitches across the canvas, always beginning on the left hand side.

SCOTTISH STITCH

Scottish stitch is also known as cushion stitch.

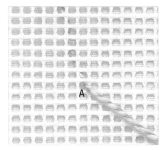

1 Secure the thread on the upper right hand side. Bring it to the front at A.

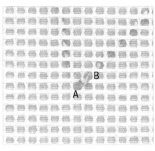

2 Crossing one canvas intersection, take the needle to the back at B, above and to the right. Pull the thread through.

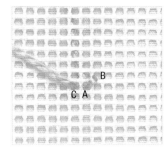

3 Re-emerge at C, one canvas thread to the left of A. Pull the thread through.

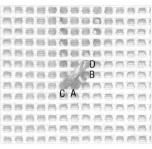

4 Take the needle to the back at D, one canvas thread above B. Pull the thread through.

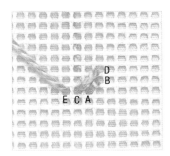

5 Re-emerge at E, one canvas thread to the left of C. Pull the thread through.

6 Take the needle to the back at F, one canvas thread above D. Pull the thread through.

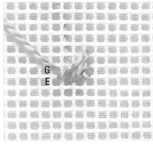

7 Re-emerge at G, one canvas thread above E. Pull the thread through.

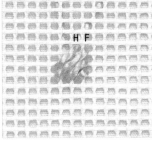

8 Take the needle to the back at H, one canvas thread to the left of F. Pull the thread through.

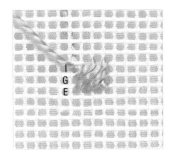

9 Re-emerge at I, one canvas thread above G. Pull the thread through.

10 Take the needle to the back at J, one canvas thread to the left of H. Pull the thread through.

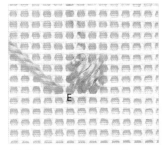

11 To begin the second Scottish stitch, bring the thread to the front one canvas thread to the left of E. Pull the thread through.

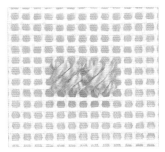

12 Work this second stitch following steps 2–10. Take care not to split the thread in the shared holes on the right hand side.

SCOTTISH STITCH / CONTINUED

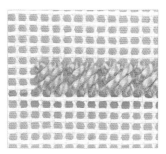

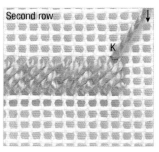

13 Working from right to left, continue working stitches across the row.

14 Turn the canvas upside down. Bring the needle to the front K.

15 Working from right to left, work stitches across the row in the same manner as the first row. Take care not to split the thread in the shared holes.

16 Continue working rows of stitches in the same manner, turning the canvas after each one.

SHELL STITCH

Shell stitch is worked in three stages.

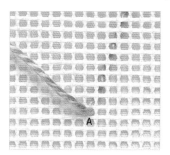

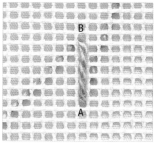

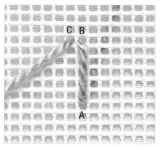

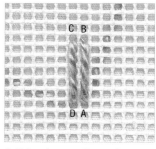

1 Secure the thread. Bring it to the front at A, on the upper right hand side.

2 Take the needle to the back at B, six canvas threads above A. Pull the thread through.

3 Re-emerge at C, one canvas thread to the left of B. Pull the thread through.

4 Take the needle to the back at D, one canvas thread to the left of A. Pull the thread through.

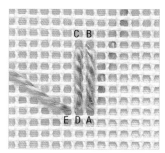

5 Re-emerge at E, one canvas thread to the left of D. Pull the thread through.

6 Take the needle to the back at F, one canvas thread to the left of C. Pull the thread through.

7 Re-emerge at G, one canvas thread to the left of F. Pull the thread through.

8 Take the needle to the back at H, one canvas thread to the left of E. Pull the thread through.

↑ Indicates top of canvas

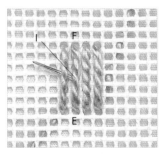

9 Re-emerge at I, halfway between E and F. Slide the needle behind the vertical stitches so it emerges to the left of all stitches.

10 Pull the thread through. Slide the needle from right to left behind all four vertical stitches. Do not go through the canvas.

11 Pull the thread through. On the right hand side, take the needle behind the stitches and to the back at J, one canvas thread to the right of I.

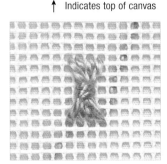

12 Pull the thread through.

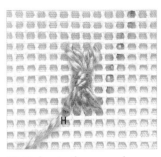

13 To begin the second stitch, bring the thread to the front at H.

14 Work the second stitch following steps 2–12.

15 Continue working stitches from right to left across the row in the same manner.

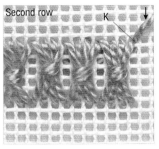

16 Turn the canvas upside down. Bring the needle to the front through the same hole as the upper right hand end of the last stitch (K). Pull the thread through.

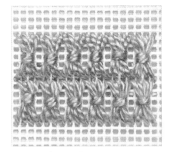

17 Work stitches across the row in the same manner as before.

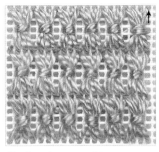

18 Continue working rows of stitches, turning the canvas after each one.

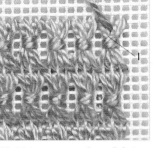

19 Using a new thread, bring it to the front at I. Come up behind the small straight stitches, emerging from the top of these stitches. Pull the thread through.

20 Slide the needle, from top to bottom, behind the second set of horizontal stitches. Do not go through the canvas.

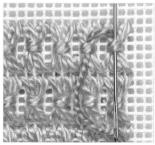

21 Pull the thread through. Slide the needle, from bottom to top, behind the first set of horizontal stitches. Do not go through the canvas.

22 Pull the thread through. Again, slide the needle, from top to bottom, behind the second set of horizontal stitches. Do not go through the canvas. Pull the thread through.

23 Slide the needle, from bottom to top, behind the third set of horizontal stitches. Do not go through the canvas.

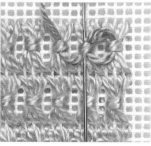

24 Pull the thread through. Again, slide the needle, from top to bottom, behind the second set of horizontal stitches. Do not go through the canvas.

25 Pull the thread through. Again, slide the needle, from bottom to top, behind the third set of horizontal stitches. Do not go through the canvas. Pull the thread through.

26 Continue in this manner to the end of the row. Each pair of horizontal stitches has 1½ coils of thread through them.

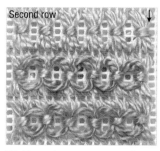

27 Turn the canvas upside down. Stitch across the row in the same manner as before.

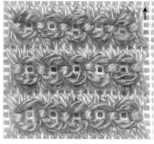

28 Continue working across each row in the same manner, turning the canvas after each one.

29 Use a new thread. Emerge at E, two canvas threads to the left of the right hand end of the last stitch in the first row. Pull the thread through.

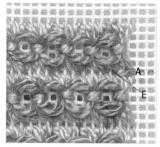

30 Take it to the back at A, two canvas threads to the right of E. Pull the thread through.

31 Bring the needle to the front two canvas threads to the left of E. Pull the thread through.

32 Take the needle to the back at E. Pull the thread through to form a back stitch.

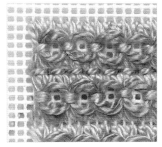

33 Continue working back stitches across the row, ensuring each stitch covers two canvas threads.

34 Turn the canvas upside down. Bring the thread to the front two canvas threads in from the right hand end and between the next two rows of sheaves.

35 Work stitches across the row in the same manner as before.

36 Continue working rows of stitches, turning the canvas after each one.

SMYRNA STITCH, STAR EYELET STITCH

See Leviathan stitch on pages 76–77.

STEM STITCH

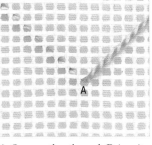

1 Secure the thread. Bring it to the front at A, on the upper left hand side.

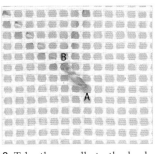

2 Take the needle to the back at B, two canvas intersections above and to the left of A. Pull the thread through.

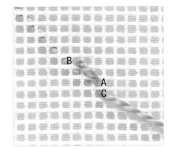

3 Re-emerge at C, one canvas thread below A. Pull the thread through.

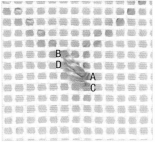

4 Take the needle to the back at D, one canvas thread below B. Pull the thread through.

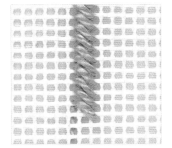

5 Continue working stitches down the row in the same manner.

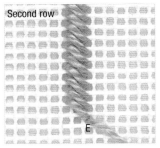

6 Bring the needle to the front through the same hole as the lower end of the last stitch (E). Pull the thread through.

STEM STITCH / CONTINUED

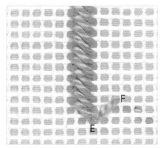

7 Take the needle to the back at F, two canvas intersections above and to the right of E. Pull the thread through.

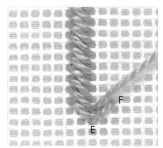

8 Re-emerge one canvas thread above E. Pull the thread through.

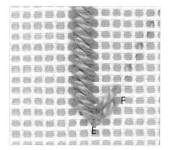

9 Take the needle to the back one canvas thread above F. Pull the thread through.

10 Continue working stitches up the row in the same manner.

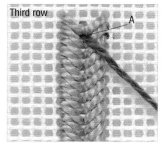

11 To begin the third row, bring the needle to the front at A. Pull the thread through.

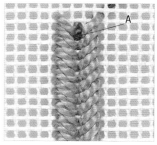

12 Take the needle to the back, one canvas thread above A. Pull the thread through.

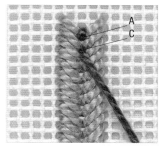

13 Re-emerge at C, one canvas thread below A. Pull the thread through.

14 Take the needle to the back at A again. Pull the thread through to form a back stitch.

15 Continue working back stitches down the row in the same manner.

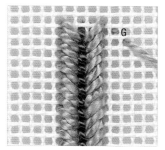

16 Return to the top to begin the second sequence of stitches. Bring the thread to the front at G, two canvas intersections below and to the right of the upper end of the last diagonal stitch.

17 Repeat the sequence following steps 2–15.

18 Continue working rows of stitches up and down the canvas.

SURREY STITCH

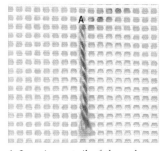

1 Leaving a tail of thread on the front, take the thread from front to back at the position for the first stitch (A).

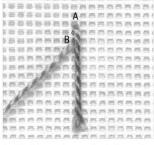

2 Holding the tail of thread to the right, bring the thread to the front at B, two canvas threads below A.

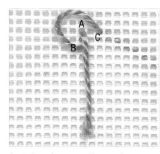

3 Take the needle to the back at C, two canvas threads to the right of A. Pull the thread through, leaving a loop.

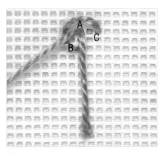

4 Re-emerge at A again, ensuring the thread from B–C is above the needle.

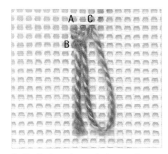

5 Pull the thread through. Take the needle to the back at C. Pull the thread through leaving a loop on the front.

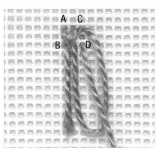

6 Re-emerge at D, two canvas threads below C and inside the loop. Pull the thread through, taking care to maintain the loop.

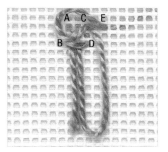

7 With the thread above the needle, take the needle to the back at E, two canvas threads to the right of C. Partially pull the thread through, taking care to maintain the loop.

8 Re-emerge at C again, ensuring the thread from D–E is above the needle. Pull the thread through.

9 Continue across the row following steps 5–8.

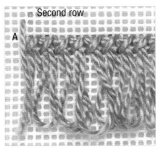

10 Return to the left hand side and take the needle to the back two canvas threads above A. Pull the thread through, leaving a tail.

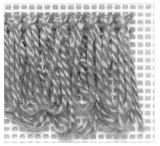

11 Work stitches, from left to right, across the row in the same manner as before.

12 Continue working rows of stitches across the canvas, always beginning on the left hand side.

TENT STITCH

See Basketweave stitch on page 16, Continental stitch on pages 28–29 and Half cross stitch on pages 33–34.

Cutting looped stitches

Looped stitches such as Rya, Surrey and Velvet stitch can all be cut and combed into a plush, luxurious pile. To do this, hold the loops upright and away from the canvas with your fingers. Trim the tops from the loops. Comb the loops with a fine comb such as an eyebrow comb. Alternate between trimming and combing until the surface is the desired height and appearance.

TRIANGLE STITCH

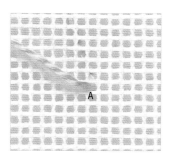

1 Secure the thread. Bring it to the front at A, on the upper left hand side.

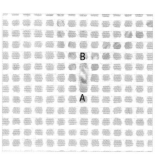

2 Take the needle to the back at B, two canvas threads above A. Pull the thread through.

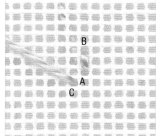

3 Re-emerge at C, one canvas intersection below and to the left of A. Pull the thread through.

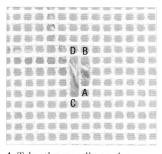

4 Take the needle to the back at D, one canvas thread to the left of B. Pull the thread through.

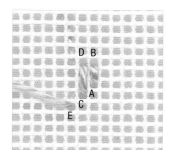

5 Re-emerge at E, one canvas intersection below and to the left of C. Pull the thread through.

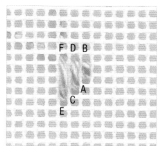

6 Take the needle to the back at F, one canvas thread to the left of D. Pull the thread through.

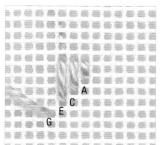

7 Re-emerge at G, one canvas intersection below and to the left of E. Pull the thread through.

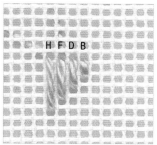

8 Take the needle to the back at H, one canvas thread to the left of F. Pull the thread through.

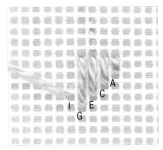

9 Re-emerge at I, one canvas intersection above and to the left of G. Pull the thread through.

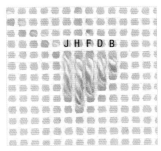

10 Take the needle to the back at J, one canvas thread to the left of H. Pull the thread through.

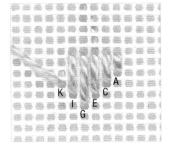

11 Re-emerge at K, one canvas intersection above and to the left of I. Pull the thread through.

12 Take the needle to the back at L, one canvas thread to the left of J. Pull the thread through.

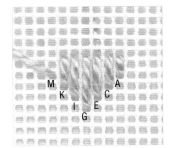

13 Re-emerge at M, one canvas intersection above and to the left of K. Pull the thread through.

14 Take the needle to the back at N, one canvas thread to the left of L. Pull the thread through.

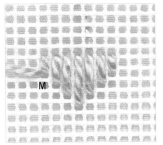

15 To work the second triangle of stitches, bring the thread to the front at M again. Pull the thread through.

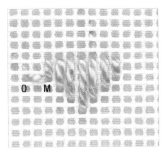

16 Take the needle to the back at O, two canvas threads to the left of M. Pull the thread through.

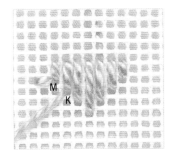

17 Re-emerge at K, one canvas thread below and to the right of M. Pull the thread through.

18 Take the needle to the back at P, one canvas thread below O. Pull the thread through.

19 Work five more stitches downwards, stitching in a similar manner as before to create a triangle.

20 To begin a third triangle of stitches, bring the needle to the front through the same hole as the right hand end of the last stitch. Pull the thread through.

21 Working from left to right, stitch the triangle in a similar manner to before.

22 To begin a fourth triangle of stitches, bring the needle to the front through the same hole as the upper end of the last stitch. Pull the thread through.

23 Working upwards, stitch the triangle in a similar manner to before.

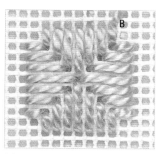

24 Bring the needle to the front at B. Pull the thread through.

25 Take the needle to the back through the right hand end of the last stitch. Pull the thread through.

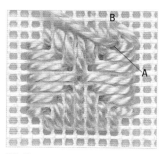

26 Re-emerge at A. Pull the thread through.

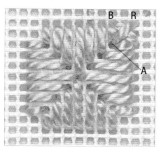

27 Crossing two canvas intersections, take the needle to the back at R, above and to the right. Pull the thread through.

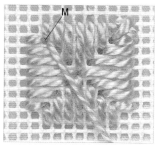

28 Bring the thread to the front at M. Pull the thread through.

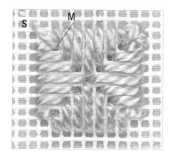

29 Crossing two canvas intersections, take the needle to the back at S, above and to the left. Pull the thread through.

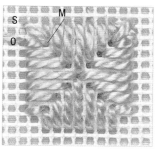

30 Re-emerge at O. Pull the thread through.

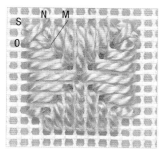

31 Take the needle to the back at N. Pull the thread through.

32 Bring the needle to the front through the same hole as the lower end of the first stitch of the third triangle. Pull the thread through.

TRIANGLE STITCH / CONTINUED

33 Crossing two canvas intersections, take the needle to the back, above and to the left. Pull the thread through.

34 Re-emerge two canvas threads below. Pull the thread through.

35 Crossing two canvas intersections, take the needle to the back, above and to the right. Pull the thread through.

36 Bring the needle to the front two canvas threads to the right of the base of the last stitch in the third triangle. Pull the thread through.

37 Crossing two canvas intersections, take the needle to the back, above and to the left. Pull the thread through.

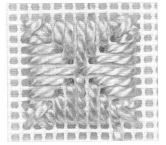

38 Re-emerge two canvas threads below. Pull the thread through.

39 Crossing two canvas intersections, take the needle to the back, above and to the right. Pull the thread through.

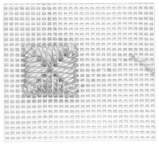

40 To begin the second triangle stitch, bring the thread to the front ten canvas threads to the right of A. Pull the thread through.

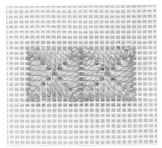

41 Work the second triangle stitch following steps 2–39.

42 Continue working stitches from left to right across the row in the same manner.

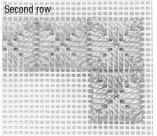

43 Work the second row, from right to left, in the same manner as before.

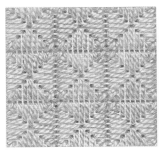

44 Continue working rows of stitches, back and forth, across the canvas.

TWEED STITCH

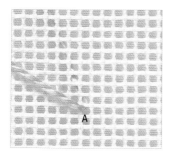

1 Secure the thread. Bring it to the front at A, on the upper left hand side.

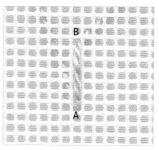

2 Take the needle to the back at B, six canvas threads above A. Pull the thread through.

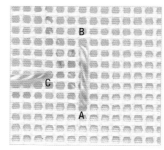

3 Re-emerge at C, three canvas threads to the left and three canvas threads below B. Pull the thread through.

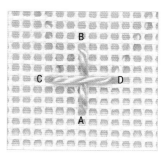

4 Take the needle to the back at D, six canvas thread to the right of C. Pull the thread through.

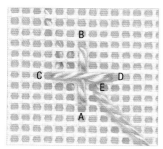

5 Re-emerge at E, two canvas threads to the left and one canvas thread below D. Pull the thread through.

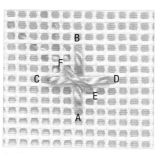

6 Crossing two canvas intersections, take the needle to the back at F, above and to the left of E. Pull the thread through.

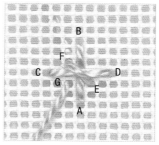

7 Re-emerge at G, two canvas threads below F. Pull the thread through.

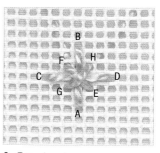

8 Crossing two canvas intersections, take the needle to the back at H, above and to the right of G. Pull the thread through.

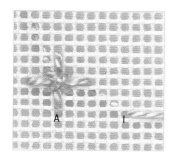

9 To begin the second stitch, bring the needle to the front at I, six canvas threads to the right of A. Pull the thread through.

10 Work this second stitch following steps 2–8.

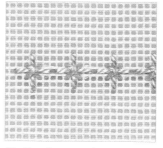

11 Continue working stitches, from left to right across the row, in the same manner.

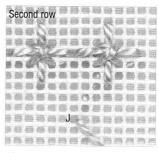

12 Bring the needle to the front three canvas threads to the left and three canvas threads below the lower end of the last stitch (J). Pull the thread through.

13 Working from right to left, stitch across the row in the same manner as before.

14 Continue working rows of stitches back and forth across the canvas.

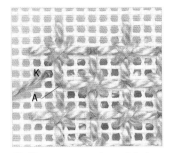

15 Using a new thread, bring it to the front at K, one canvas intersection above and to the left of A. Pull the thread through.

16 Take the needle to the back at L, one canvas intersection above and to the left of K. Pull the thread through.

17 Re-emerge at M, one canvas thread below L. Pull the thread through.

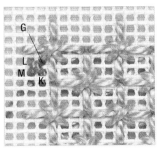

18 Take the needle to the back at G, one canvas intersection above and to the right of M. Pull the thread through.

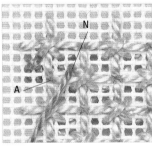

19 To begin the second small cross stitch, bring the thread to the front at N, two canvas threads to the right and one above A.

20 Work this stitch following steps 16–18.

21 Continue working stitches, from left to right, across the row in the same manner.

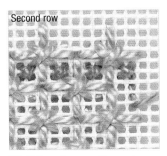

22 Bring the needle to the front three canvas threads below the lower right corner of the previous cross stitch. Pull the thread through.

23 Work stitches, from right to left, across the row in the same manner as before.

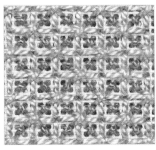

24 Continue working rows of tiny cross stitches, back and forth, across the canvas.

VEE STITCH

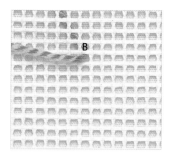

1 Secure the thread on the upper left hand side. Bring it to the front at B.

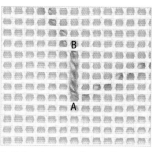

2 Take the needle to the back at A, four canvas threads below B. Pull the thread through.

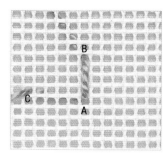

3 Re-emerge at C, five canvas threads to the left and one above A. Pull the thread through.

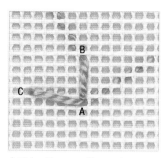

4 Take the needle to the back at A again. Pull the thread through.

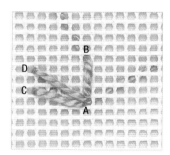

5 Re-emerge at D, two canvas threads above C. Take the needle to the back at A again. Pull the thread through.

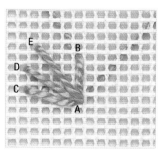

6 Re-emerge at E, two canvas threads above and one to the right of D. Take the needle to the back at A again. Pull the thread through.

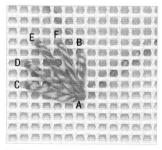

7 Re-emerge at F, two canvas threads to the right of E. Take the needle to the back at A again. Pull the thread through.

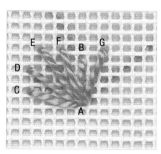

8 Re-emerge at G, four canvas threads to the right of F. Take the needle to the back at A again. Pull the thread through.

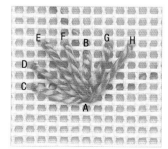

9 Re-emerge at H, two canvas threads to the right of G. Take the needle to the back at A again. Pull the thread through.

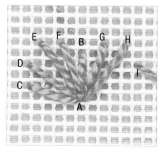

10 Re-emerge at I, two canvas threads below and one to the right of H. Take the needle to the back at A again. Pull the thread through.

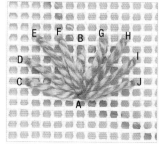

11 Re-emerge at J, two canvas threads below I. Take the needle to the back at A again. Pull the thread through.

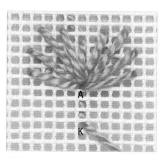

12 To begin the second stitch, bring the needle to the front at K, four canvas threads below A. Pull the thread through.

13 Take the needle to the back at A. Pull the thread through.

14 Re-emerge at L, five canvas threads to the left and one above K. Take the needle to the back at K again. Pull the thread through.

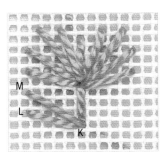

15 Re-emerge at M, two canvas threads above L. Take the needle to the back at K again. Pull the thread through.

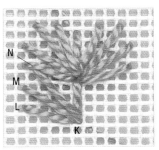

16 Re-emerge at N, two canvas threads above and one to the right of M. Take the needle to the back at K again. Pull the thread through.

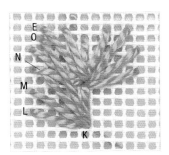

17 Re-emerge at O, one canvas thread below E. Take the needle to the back at K again. Pull the thread through.

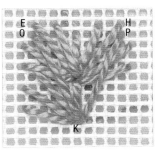

18 Re-emerge at P, one canvas thread below H. Take the needle to the back at K again. Pull the thread through.

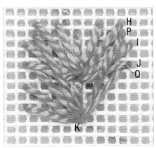

19 Re-emerge at Q, one canvas thread to the left of J. Take the needle to the back at K again. Pull the thread through.

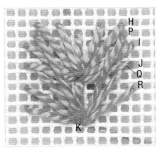

20 Re-emerge at R, two canvas threads below and one to the right of Q. Take the needle to the back at K again. Pull the thread through.

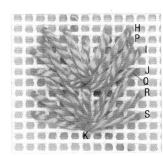

21 Re-emerge at S, two canvas threads below R. Take the needle to the back at K again. Pull the thread through.

22 To begin the third stitch, bring the needle to the front four canvas threads below K. Pull the thread through.

23 Work this stitch following steps 13–21.

24 Continue working stitches down the row in the same manner.

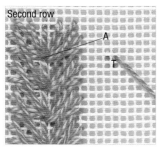

25 Return to the top of the canvas. Bring the needle to the front at T, nine canvas threads to the right of A. Pull the thread through.

26 Work the first stitch of this row following steps 2–11. The first two diagonal stitches slightly overlap the previous row.

27 Work the second stitch following steps 13–21. Continue in this manner to the end of the row.

28 Continue working rows in the same manner, always returning to the top of the canvas to begin each one.

VELVET STITCH

Velvet stitch is also known as Astrakhan stitch.

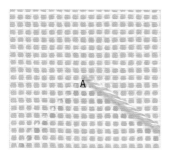

1 Secure the thread on the lower left hand side. Bring it to the front at A.

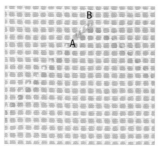

2 Crossing two canvas intersections, take the needle to the back at B, above and to the right. Pull the thread through.

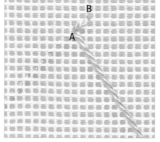

3 Re-emerge at A again. Pull the thread through.

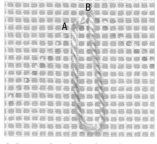

4 Loop the thread to the right and hold in place. Take the needle to the back at B again. Pull the thread through.

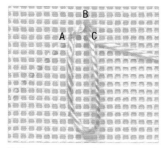

5 Re-emerge at C, two canvas threads below B and to the right of the loop. Still holding the loop, pull the thread through.

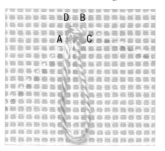

6 Take the needle to the back at D, two canvas threads above A. Pull the thread through.

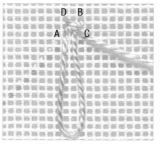

7 To begin the second stitch, bring the needle to the front at C. Pull the thread through.

8 Work this second stitch following steps 2–6.

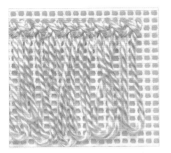

9 Working from left to right, continue working stitches across the row.

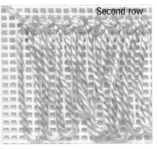

10 Return to the left hand side and bring the needle to the front at D. Pull the thread through.

11 Work stitches, from left to right, across the row in the same manner as before.

12 Continue working rows of stitches across the canvas, always beginning on the left hand side.

WEB STITCH

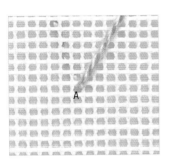

1 Secure the thread on the upper left hand side. Bring it to the front at A.

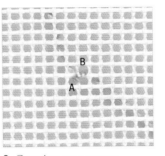

2 Crossing one canvas intersection, take the needle to the back at B, above and to the right. Pull the thread through.

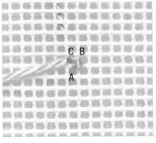

3 Re-emerge at C, one canvas thread above A. Pull the thread through.

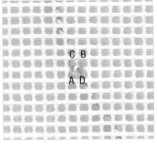

4 Take the needle to the back at D, one canvas intersection below and to the right of C. Pull the thread through.

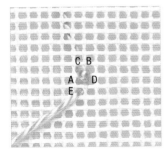

5 Re-emerge at E, one canvas thread below A. Pull the thread through.

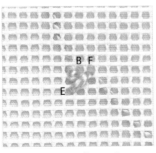

6 Take the needle to the back at F, one canvas thread to the right of B. Pull the thread through.

7 Re-emerge at B, one canvas thread to the left of F. Pull the thread through.

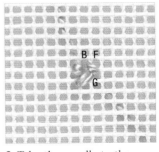

8 Take the needle to the back at G, one canvas intersection below and to the right of B. Pull the thread through.

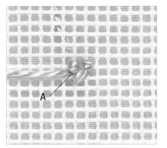

9 Re-emerge at A, again. Pull the thread through.

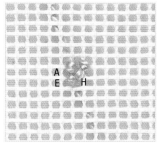

10 Take the needle to the back at H, one canvas intersection below and to the right of A. Pull the thread through.

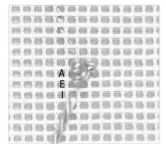

11 Bring the thread to the front at I, one canvas thread below E. Pull the thread through.

12 Take the needle to the back at J, one canvas thread to the right of F. Pull the thread through.

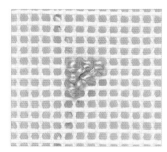

13 Couch this long thread at every canvas intersection in the same manner as before.

14 Beginning on the left hand side and finishing on the top side, work a long diagonal straight stitch as before.

15 Couch this long thread at every canvas intersection in the same manner as before.

16 Continue working long diagonal straight stitches and couching them at each canvas intersection until the desired space is filled.

WHEATSHEAF STITCH

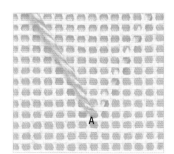

1 Secure the thread. Bring it to the front at A, on the upper right hand side.

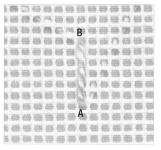

2 Take the needle to the back at B, six canvas threads above A. Pull the thread through.

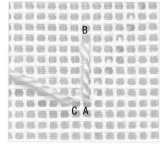

3 Re-emerge at C, one canvas thread to the left of A. Pull the thread through.

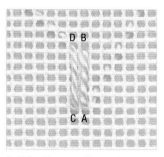

4 Take the needle to the back at D, one canvas thread to the left of B. Pull the thread through.

↑ Indicates top of canvas

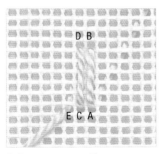

5 Re-emerge at E, one canvas thread to the left of C. Pull the thread through.

6 Take the needle to the back at F, one canvas thread to the left of D. Pull the thread through.

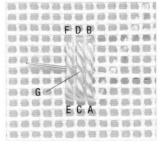

7 Bring the needle to the front at G, halfway between C and D. Slide the needle behind the vertical stitches so it emerges to the left of all stitches.

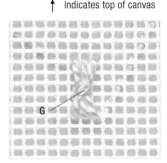

8 Pull the thread through. Slide the needle from right to left behind the vertical stitches and to the back at G. Pull the thread through.

9 To begin the second stitch, bring the needle to the front at H, one canvas thread to the left of E. Pull the thread through.

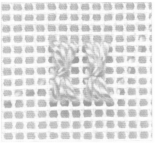

10 Work the second stitch following steps 2–8.

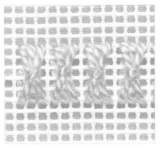

11 Continue working stitches, from right to left across the row, in the same manner.

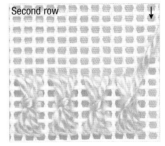

12 Turn the canvas upside down. Bring the needle to the front through the same hole as the upper right hand corner of the previous stitch.

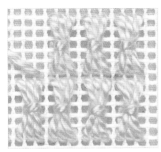

13 Work stitches, from right to left across the row in the same manner as before.

14 Continue working rows of stitches, turning the canvas after each one.

Detail of french needlework furniture covering, 1720

Index

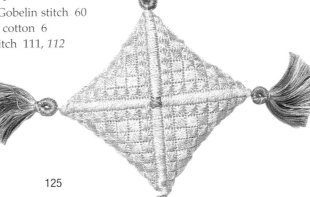

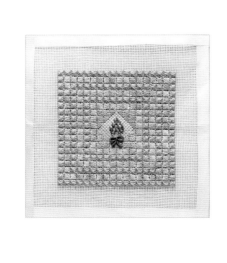